Karen
Thank you
being part of my
Journey

Nomad's Search
for Freedom

Reconciling with Destiny's path

C.C. Dorrie

Copyright © 2016, C.C. Dorrie
www.ccdorrie.com

All rights reserved. No part of this publication may be reproduced, dis-
tributed, or transmitted in any form or by any means, including photo-
copying, recording, or other electronic or mechanical methods, without
the prior written permission of the publisher, except in the case of brief
quotations embodied in critical reviews and certain other noncommer-
cial uses permitted by copyright law.

ISBN: 0995190119
ISBN 13: 9780995190115
Editing by Sylvia Cottrell @ Ex-Libris Editing
Book cover design by Tatjana Vukoja
Additional support by Create Space

I have tried to recreate events, locales and conversations from my memories of them. While all the stories in this book are true, In order to maintain their anonymity in some instances I have changed the names of individuals and places, I may have changed some identifying characteristics and details such as physical properties, occupations and places of residence.

I am dedicating this book to my mother, who is my best friend and the strongest person I know. To my husband, whose unabridged support made this work possible. To my boys, may they never live through the same nightmares I have, and may they always keep their joie de vivre—*their sense of wonder—in their hearts. I hope one day they will understand why I am the mother they received, and that they forgive my mistakes.*

Acknowledgements

First and foremost, I want to humbly thank my mother who remains my best friend to this day and who found ways beyond her means to help me finance this book. She will forever be my "rock". Secondly, I wish to thank my sister, for her unconditional support and contributions to our mother's successful endeavors, as well as to mine.

I want to thank my kids as well as my husband, Koko, whose constant love and support throughout this trying and strenuous process, during which emotions were frequently on edge, compelled me to reach beyond the stars.

I would like to thank my charismatic good friend Que from DCL, who stood me in front of that mirror_ thank you. To my friend Nicole Foret Oberleitner, from RSSN, whose decision to ask me to be a part of her fundraiser, revealed a branch on my destiny's tree that was previously hidden from view. To Caryna Khan, my beloved Aussie entrepreneur whose tremendous support from across the globe has been nothing but genuine and enthusiastic.

I would also like to thank all of the people who have contributed to the making of this book by numerous means, whether on the more technical side of things or in the broader area of support and encouragement. Thank you Kenny, Nathalie, Nadia and Steven, Lesley, Cindy Harrie, Mel, Jennie, and Dan. This wonderful group of people's love, enthusiasm and reassurance, as well as their pure belief in the deep rooted message of this book, made this endeavor possible. I also want to thank my devoted, kind, and extremely talented editor, Sylvia Cottrell, who took my words and made them shine.

Last but not least, thank you to Gigi and Ralph; my Angels sent from up above.

Preface

My ultimate goal with this book is to help people of all ages to overcome their obstacles and to believe that their existence is valid despite having suffered horrible circumstances—circumstances that can be overcome by carving out an authentic, blissful place in society.

You do not need to be a victim nor a conformist. Take your place in the world. Be who you were meant to be. Believe that, no matter what has happened in your life in the past or is happening in your life now, you are strong enough to survive it. Someone chose *you* to bear these scars for some reason. Perhaps you will never know the true "why," but it is up to you to determine which road you will take with your burdens.

Grieve, cry, curse the skies if you need to, talk to someone if you want to—and then find a way to turn the page on that chapter, to let it go, to release it into the universe. Become a source of inspiration for others, and you will see that your sorrows, regardless of how deep they run, will soon be replaced by the joy of helping another human being. If you only help one person through your story, you have done more than most will ever do.

The choice is always yours to make, and I hope that you choose the right path for you, free of heaviness. There are always crossroads in our lives, and it is up to us to take responsibility for our own happiness when we reach these crossroads. We must never blame others, because ultimately we must make the choice to be happy regardless of who has wronged us. If you continue to live in blame, you are giving the person or people who have wronged you more power than they deserve.

Table of Contents

Introduction: Angels

I don't know why it happened that particular year, but it was in June of 2002 that I made peace with the ghosts of my past.

Well, that's not actually 100% true. I didn't do it on my own. It happened with a little help from my German angel—about whom you will learn more later—who helped me to open the undeniable Pandora's box and face the demons lurking within.

Everyone has their own story to tell, and I've decided to share mine. This is a story—one that belongs to both myself and to my mother—about being bruised, battered, and broken. It's a story of finding a way to pick up the pieces and move forward despite the odds, not knowing where we would end up or if we would even make it there alive. It's a story about being willing to risk everything you know in the name of something better, in the name of freedom.

Throughout this narrative, I use my voice to tell my side of the story and as close to my mother's voice as possible to tell hers—revealed with our hearts and souls and as candid as we can possibly be—to give others hope. Across our years of separation and through those spent as inseparable best friends, my mother and I both survived the storms of destiny's path and succeeded to find happiness, laughter, and to live fulfilling lives.

Now, I am not the smartest person in the universe. I didn't reinvent the wheel or anything else for that matter, I am not a doctor nor a lawyer nor a priest, but I do have my tumultuous life as an offering to share with others who are weathering their own storms. I was brought into this world with many challenges ahead of me, but at the end of it all, I succeeded to find my "happily ever after"—and even to come out somewhat normal!

The story that brought me to where I am now—living in a peaceful Oceanside town on the east coast of Canada—is anything but peaceful. It is tumultuous, heart-rending, and sometimes almost unimaginable.

At the tender age of eight, my father abducted me from our small town in Communist Slovakia. That day, I began my life as a nomad, constantly on the move from one country and city to the next. Over time, I found comfort and a sense of adventure in the shifting nature of meeting new people and basking in the wonder of the forever-changing scenery around me. As a young adult, I sought freedom through a stream of moves, jobs, and new relationships all over the world. And yet, I still didn't feel free. It wasn't until more than twenty years after my abduction, while soaking in the sun on the idyllic sandy beaches of Santorini, that I discovered true freedom; the kind that originates from within when you allow yourself to honor and heal on destiny's path.

I decided to share our story so that you too can find your way and your peace if you are searching for these things. Some will search hopelessly all of their lives, but for others who are more open to change, perhaps they will find their path—as I did—with a little help from an angel or two along the way.

Everyone has angels. They come into our lives unexpected, gently redirecting us and showing us the way to our new path. You just have to know how to call them and especially how to welcome them without hesitation toward the new, toward the beautiful, and toward the harmony that didn't make its way in our lives previously because we were busy elsewhere—namely with our misery.

It is my hope that, with the help of the angels in your life, you are one day able to find real freedom as I have and to heal from the traumas of your past by walking the true path of your destiny.

Part One

Tumultuous Years

A Mother's Worst Nightmare: Hnusta, Slovakia — 1981

Under the watchful eyes of the residents of the little village of Hnusta, two tall men dressed in black suits—long black coats to their calves, black fedoras pulled low on their brows—approached the gas station that my mother managed. You could make out their twin cold, smileless faces from afar. No introductions necessary.

KGB.

Wherever agents of the KGB went, fear reigned. They were the omnipresent watchdog of the Communist beast that ruled our lives. When they arrived, no one ever wanted to cause trouble, so most would obey and stay quiet like good little soldiers to avoid being targeted themselves. Those who didn't were brutally interrogated or surveilled by bugs planted in their homes. Educated citizens were made to perform menial tasks like sweeping streets, and some people were taken by the KGB, never to be seen again—branded as traitors and transferred to merciless, bitter Siberia because they'd dared to voice their discontent on matters such as politics or food shortages. Others were sent to uranium mines or simply dumped in prisons where many didn't last long. Some were taken away because a brother or sister or parent, in hopes of keeping the family together, had snitched on a loved one who was planning to escape. They were shown no mercy.

Slowly, the small crowd surrounding my mother's place of work dispersed as the men drew closer.

"Mrs. Laskova," one of the men said when they'd reached the station, "did you know that your husband has escaped across the border with your daughter?"

"No, it cannot be true!" she replied, her face pale and shock plain in her voice. Her worst nightmare had just become a reality.

My mothers' good looks and charm were no match against the KGB agents. She was a stunning, petite woman with the most beautiful green eyes and thick, wavy hair down to her shoulders. She was always elegantly dressed considering the times, and was loved by everyone not only because of her naively kind heart but also because of her position working at the gas station. It seems silly for us here in the West—that such a position could be reputable—but growing up in Communist Slovakia it was a privilege to work in a gas station, since many shenanigans could easily be conducted there and extra money could be made from tipping customers.

My mother stared at the agents. Her father had been right. My father Caesar had indeed taken me on a vacation some years before, but this was not abnormal. The fact that I hadn't returned was.

"He will take her!" my grandfather had told her only weeks earlier. "Don't let her go with him. He will steal her." My mother had dismissed her father's concerns out of pure denial. "He will, you watch!" her father had said in desperation, struggling against his leukemia symptoms—a disease that would eventually claim his life.

But how could he? Why would he? Those answers took six suspenseful, fearsome months of waiting to be revealed.

— —

It was only two days before the KGB arrived at my mother's gas station that she and her best friend, Helena, had been trying to find out where I was. I hadn't returned from my "vacation" with my father, so she decided to go to my father's mother's village, in Lucenec, around 50 kilometers from Hnusta. With a whole bunch of candy in her purse, she hoped to bribe information of my whereabouts out of the neighborhood children.

Expecting that I would be hidden at his sister Dana's house, she decided to go there first. A kind, intelligent woman with short hair and dark eyes, Dana had a pure and immeasurable love for me and used to call me (and still does to this day) *laska velikanska*, which means "my great love."

Now, a couple of years after my birth, my father offered
my mother a deal. He asked her if she would be alright with
selling me, his own daughter, for the amount of 10,000
Koruna—not even $500 in Canadian dollars—to Dana.
I've never been sure where that wicked idea came from; I
guess he wanted to help his sister, who couldn't have any
children of her own. At least that's how I decided to see it.
My poor mother told him that he was crazy and refused to
give me up—thus the reasoning behind why she decided to
go and see if my father had hid me in Dana's house.

"Hey kids," my mother said to the children playing
in the street outside my aunt's house when she arrived,
"did you see a little girl with short hair that looks like
a boy around here playing?" She handed out pieces of
candy and tried to look friendly and not desperate while
showing the children a picture of me.

"Yes, we did!" they answered jovially, having recognized my face from the times we'd played together before. The children continued to play, oblivious to the
seriousness of the situation.

"Oh, good," my mother replied, relieved. "So where
is she? Is she here now?"

"No," one of the children said, and my mother's
stomach dropped in panic. "We saw her...um...it was
about two months ago."

She thanked the children and decided to make her way
to her mother-in-law's house, which was at the end of the
village and not too far from Dana's. The hatred between
my mother and my father's mother was mutual, but she

put her pride aside and went anyway. My father's mother was a mean-spirited woman who regularly excused my father's many affairs and despicable behavior toward my mother and me. Thankfully, my mother's father-in-law, with whom she had a much better relationship, answered the call of the doorbell.

"Is my daughter here?" she asked him immediately, desperation in her voice.

"No, neither she nor he is here. They didn't come back from the vacation they took." Her worry was reflected on his face. As they spoke, Dana arrived.

"We are so worried, we don't know where they are," she said once she'd heard my mother's concerns. "He didn't write, didn't call—we have no idea where they are... no idea if they are dead or alive...we know nothing!" she cried. My mother realized that Dana was telling the truth. The pain and worry was much too obvious in her eyes for her to be lying.

My mother left the village with more questions than answers, but she was still hopeful that we were actually somewhere in a hospital, or that we had decided to travel a little longer in the surrounding countries. Knowing that this was likely wishful thinking, however, she chose to call my father's boss to see if he knew anything.

"Where is Caesar? He didn't come back from his vacation. We have to call the police! He should have come back by now," she said when she got him on the line.

"No, Mrs. Laskova, why don't we wait a little longer, eh? Maybe they are in a hospital—maybe the little one got sick, or he got sick, or perhaps they went to Bulgaria? Let's not panic and wait another week." His words were not reassuring, but what could she do?

"Okay, maximum a week, and then I will go to the police."

Days passed, and still no word reached her from my father or me. And then the day came—two men in dark coats and hats approached her gas station, and she knew they could only bring bad news.

The two KGB agents recounted what they knew about my whereabouts to my mother, who listened in growing horror and disbelief.

"Yes, it's true. They've escaped. The last traces they left were from when they crossed the Yugoslavian-Greek border. The rest we don't know."

My mother was silent.

"Did you know that he was going to escape?" one of the agents pressed.

"Of course not," my mother said. "He has my daughter! I would have never given her to him if I'd known he was planning to escape. We are divorced, and she is in my custody. He was supposed to just take her on a vacation…." She broke down in sobs, still in pure shock.

"Well, if you hear from them, we expect you to let us know," one of them said as they were leaving, unaffected by my mother's agony. The fact that my father had dared to leave the country with me without authorization was of much greater concern to them than a family being torn apart.

But it was too late for anyone to do anything, anyway. We were long gone.

The Lost Child

"Vacation"

I sat in a filthy bathroom on an old-fashioned train—a train that was hurtling toward who knew where. I, for one, had no idea.

My father, to put it bluntly, was a classic womanizer. He was smooth, tall, and handsome—slim but muscular with short, curly hair. He was extremely book-smart, and a great conversationalist when he wanted to be. He used all of this to his advantage with people—especially women. He told me to go and stay in the washroom of the dirty old train for a while. Since I was an extremely docile child, I listened to him and went. I sat there, watching the mountains pass me by and trying to block out the sewer-like stench.

I stayed there for what seemed like a long time. While I was in hiding, my father's plan was to make friends with the Greek people who were traveling in the same wagon with us in the hopes of them helping him with the

Sluzba Drzavne Bezbednosti (SDB), or the State Security Service, which was one of the many "watch dog" divisions of the KGB.

Caesar talked the Greek passengers up, making fast friends and gaining their trust. When the SDB got on the train to verify everyone's papers in case of potential defectors (a high number of people fleeing Communism used Yugoslavia as an escape route to a better world), my father's new friends informed the SDB that he was traveling with them.

By some miracle, it worked.

Those "friends" ended up playing a crucial role in the shaping of the rest of my life. Unknowingly, they helped my father commit one of the most unimaginably offensive crimes there is—taking a child away from her mother—and, ultimately, they also helped us escape a Communist country in a time when this was a near-impossible feat. By making the decision to vouch for him, my father's new friends he made on the train that day would change the course of my life—a course that would shatter the lives of so many as well as impact both my destiny and the destinies of those around me.

In many ways, I believe that my father kidnapped me to exact revenge on my mother for perceived wrongs. His revenge had been thoroughly planned and was brilliantly executed. It took seven years for my mother to find her way back to me. But before I tell the rest of her story, we must first journey back to my parents' painful past.

Slovakia's Not-So-Fond Memories, 1972 – 1981

Slovakia was under Communist rule from 1948 through 1989. I am not going to write a history book about those times, but suffice it to say that our government told us that the capitalist West was *bad, bad, bad* with every chance they got. Everyone had their precious belongings as well as most of their land and homes taken away from them— everything you owned belonged to the government. That included your furniture, jewelry and keepsakes, car, and livestock. The KGB rampaged through villages in the hopes of finding anyone with malicious intent toward the regime. They went from door to door to see who owned what, and made sure to let the owners know that everything was the government's property, not theirs.

Those who kept chickens in the villages had a weekly quota to give to the regime called *kontigent*, a merger of everyone's livestock. It was the same with pigs. Unfortunately, for those who owned cows and horses like my great-grandfather, their livestock was confiscated wholesale and placed in communal land plots where the original owners would go to work. This allowed the government to reap the fruits of their labor for the alleged benefit of the whole country.

The Communist regime didn't want you to be an individual. When you take that away from people, people tend to rebel, and since most couldn't rebel with words, they did so with booze instead, and alcoholism was rampant. Political prisoners were transferred to Siberia or thrown in jail—many never returned home. Some were put to work in uranium mines, their bodies slowly decaying from the various health hazards of working without any security measures.

Once male citizens received their education and gave one or two years of their lives to the regime as soldiers, the government placed the men in ugly, gray apartments that all looked the same where they would live out their lives with their wives and children if they had them. You had no choice in the matter.

We used newspaper for toilet paper. We had to wait in line outside sometimes all night to get "exotic" fruits like oranges, bananas, and watermelons. Things like jeans were frowned upon since they were considered a luxury item, and regular people couldn't really own luxury items unless you had some type of connection to get money to buy them—often in a special store called Tuzex. Those connections included family members who had escaped and would send money to their families back in Slovakia in the hopes of making their lives a little sweeter and easier. Banks would exchange the money into Slovak Koruna or Boni, but the people would never get the true value for that money once exchanged because the government would keep a cut.

We would rarely buy meat like pork or beef; approximately once a month if you were lucky. Those living in small villages in the country would have rabbits for their meat and chickens for eggs as well as for meat, and they would often send part of their bounty to their families living in the city—after handing over their quota to the regime, of course. Men went hunting for boars and deer; even bears in order to get some meat on the table.

There were never many gifts underneath our sparsely decorated Christmas trees. We were given oranges—one per child—that parents waited in line for at night. We savored those oranges for hours and were very grateful for them, some of us crying while eating them.

We were still better off than millions of our Ukrainian neighbors east of us, where most of the bourgeois had been massacred and where food was so scarce that people did unimaginable, unthinkable things to survive. Holodomor, known as the Terror-Famine in Ukraine, was a horrific genocide of the Ukrainian people by starvation where millions perished. In many ways, it feels like we lived in a kingdom in comparison.

This isn't to say our lives were filled with joy. Far from it. My family lived on the sixth floor of one of those macabre apartments I mentioned earlier. It had a dark, morbid atmosphere to it, and had been built in a village of the same. Our home looked like something from a war movie: a large, rectangular, gray cement block. The government gave my father the apartment right after he finished his lengthy education in forestry and had done his time in the army—I say "lengthy" since he flunked out of his forestry program a couple of times because he wanted to travel in the surrounding (fellow Communist) countries.

Before the apartment, we stayed for a year with my grandparents in Salkova at my mother's parents' house.

The modest two-story house was forth on a tiny street on top of a hill, with a large field behind where my grandmother would grow fruits and vegetables like wild strawberries, prunes, cherry and apple trees, beans, tomatoes, peppers, and our main source of food, potatoes, in order to stock up for winter. On the main floor, which looked more like a basement, was an outhouse. The main living area was on top.

She housed her beloved rabbits and chickens in the yard, always keeping one rabbit as her pet to mitigate the guilt of killing them. Once every seven years or so, all the rabbits got some disease that would wipe them all out, and she would have to wait for months before being able to buy herself a new mating pair to provide the much-needed protein on our tables.

We were the only ones with a television in the village, so all the villagers would gather in our modest house to watch it. The only reason we had a television was because my grandfather was an intelligent, highly respected scientist with a prestigious job. He had built himself a television from scratch.

My grandfather, who was a somewhat quiet person—a short, classy gent with black hair and blue eyes—emanated respect and was loved by everyone.

My grandmother, who worked at the pharmaceutical factory in close by Banska Bystrica, was also loved by others; however, she suffered from a hormonal condition that frequently made dealing with regular, daily situations a huge struggle for her. Flows of anger, frustration, irritability, impatience, depression, snappishness, and pure rage would come rushing through her unexpectedly, and these flashes were nearly impossible to control or overcome.

I suffer from a similar condition, but I am fortunate enough to live in a country where medical help is right at my fingertips, and thus my condition is manageable. For my grandmother, there was no help to be had. I doubt that my family knew that this "problem" existed and was manageable through medication, or even had time to wonder about it. To us, it was just how our grandmother was. She struggled blindly with it every day.

She was a hardheaded, strong woman; especially when it came to my mother, her only daughter. Out of pure rage one day, she tried throwing my mother—then only a teenager—off the balcony from the second floor of her house for the simple reason that my mother had refused to follow a "silly village tradition" called *Majak*. During the month of May, the "love" month, young boys from the village would plant birch branches during the night in the front porches of the houses where young girls lived in the village. The next morning, the young men would come back for their prize, which consisted of the girl's parents giving them some money and offering up their daughter to dance with them. My mother, who snubbed this tradition, didn't want her parents to waste money on it and decided to break the branches. My grandmother, infuriated by this defiant act, decided it was a good idea to throw my poor mother from the balcony as punishment.

Thankfully, she didn't fall, but held on by her fingertips until a neighbor could come to her aid.

My grandmother would also frequently beat my mother—a cruelty she only visited on her, for whatever reason—with anything she could find, whether it be a large wooden ladle, a belt, a hanger, thick strings of rope, or a pot. Despite this, everyone loved her for her kind, welcoming, and giving nature toward others—toward everyone but my mother, that is. My mother would come home just a minute late and would invariably be welcomed by a slap across her face.

It was in this house on top of a little hill, in this small village, where my father started to show his true colors.

While I was entering the world (a difficult birth; my mother needed emergency surgery and a transfusion), my father was in the basement of the house he shared with his wife and mother-in-law, sleeping with another woman. A nosy neighbor told my grandmother that her daughter and her husband should shut their curtains if they were going to have sex. "But my daughter is in the hospital, giving birth to my grandchild!" my grandmother replied, completely oblivious. Sadly, the act of sleeping with one of his string of lovers while his wife was in the hospital giving birth to his daughter wasn't abnormal behavior for him.

For my parents' wedding a few months before my arrival, no one but my mother's second brother, Lubo, and Janko, a friend of Caesar's, came to witness the impending disaster of their union. Lubo was the only one of my mother's siblings who could tolerate my father. He was tall with dark hair, dark eyes, and a darker complexion; the only one in a family of white-as-snow skin, blue or green eyes, and sandy hair. Lubo was my grandmother's favorite; he was the funniest, and she loved him dearly. She used to call him "my Brusnian," a reference to the place where she came from, Brusno. Lubo was always joking—he told the funniest stories and had a way about him that made everyone smitten with him within moments—including me.

My father told my mother that he wanted "authentic" wedding pictures. He accomplished this by opting not to smile as well as deciding to wear huge, circular, dark sunglasses covering half of his face—hence the "authenticity," whatever that meant for him. They wed against everyone's wishes, and it was not long after their union that my father's violent undertones came to the surface. He became more and more jealous of anyone who dared to smile at my mother, or vice versa, and things only got worse when we moved away.

Feeling safe in the sanctuary of the new apartment in Hnusta, 83 kilometers away from our old home, his purely evil ways emerged. This was the starting point of the ruthless beatings my mother would endure for the next six years.

The apartment layout was not like here in the West, as the open concept was still non-existent at the time. Each floor of the building housed three apartments: one in front and one on either side. Once you entered our apartment on the sixth floor, a long, parallel hallway led inward. At the end of the hallway to the right was a kitchen with a door, and inside the kitchen was another door leading to the washroom. Just before the kitchen was another door leading to the same small washroom.

In the middle of the hallway was another door for the terra-cotta-colored living room, which had a wall mural on the right wall of a sunset overlooking the ocean with palm trees. There was a tall, elegant vase with peacock feathers at the foot of the door. Through the living room at the far left was another bedroom. My bedroom was on the other end of the hallway, close to the entrance. All of the doors had locks on them. Considering the times in which we lived, my mother was able to make our apartment as beautiful and homey as she possibly could.

We had family that we saw from time to time—my sister from my mother's first marriage, who lived with my mothers' parents and was raised as their own daughter. My grandfather loved her massively, and he wanted to keep her with him because he said that she was the only thing that kept him going in the final stages of terminal leukemia. My mother wanted to take my sister to live with us, but he insisted on her staying with him for the remainder of his life and my mother agreed to keep him happy. We visited each other on weekends. Needless to say, my sister's experiences with my father's monstrosities were nonexistent—she had no clue of what was going on beside the fact of noticing my mother's bruised face and body when we saw each other.

My mother was a stunning woman whom many men yearned for—including my father, and to her own misfortune, she chose him. Lust and passion were the reasons for their union. But lust does not last, nor does it provide a stable foundation for a relationship, and it didn't take long for them to become enemies.

Pre-Divorce Years

My parents eventually did divorce, but for six long, dark years before they separated we lived in fear. Many nights, my father would come home beyond drunk—and drunkenness almost always meant beatings. My mother, infatuated with my father and deep in denial, believed that each beating would somehow be the last. He helped feed this hope by apologetically staring at her swollen and bruised face the next morning, putting cold compresses on her injuries and no doubt wondering who had ravaged her (without realizing it had been him).

One day, in his drunken state, my father came knocking at the living room door.

"Where is your mother?" he asked me, staggering.

"Mami, Caesar wants to see you," I warily called out to her. I was forbidden to call my father "father"—I had to call him by his name. I made the mistake of calling him

"Daddy" once, and he smacked me across the face with his strong hand and screamed, "Never call me Daddy! I am Caesar to you!" Lesson learned.

My poor mother answered my call, and out of the blue, brutally and with all of his strength, my father punched her with his right fist, just like a boxer. She flew across the living room table and fell onto the floor with blood gushing down her mouth. He hastily made his way to her immobile form and continued to punch her over and over. Any attempt to flee was met with more blows. Blood splattered everywhere around us—on the walls, on our clothes, on his fists. He kept alternating from vicious punches to the head and face to solid kicks wherever he could reach. She looked like a worm caught out in the sun after a heavy rain, writhing and trying desperately to find shelter, but there was no dark, safe place to crawl away to.

I quickly inched around them, ran through the doorway, and sprinted down two flights of stairs to the apartment of my mom's best friend, Helena, whom my father was afraid of. She may have been the only person he was afraid of. She was of small build—perhaps five foot two—but extremely strong. Helena had short, black, curly hair and dark brown eyes and was very tomboyish. She worked in a factory, smoked like a chimney, liked her red wine, and was the only woman with whom my father would reason.

I knocked at the door as loud as I dared, for in those times, a child needed to have manners regardless of the circumstances.

"Aunt Helena, Aunt Helena!" I cried, "Caesar is beating up Mommy again, come quickly!" My voice was shaking. The door opened, and Helena appeared. I pulled on her hand to follow me upstairs, thinking that if anyone could stop this madness, it would be her. We ran upstairs and she firmly told me to wait right outside the door while she went to "reason" with him—or beat him senseless, I hoped.

Things quieted down after a couple of minutes, and then I had clearance to go back in again. My mother, her face somewhat cleaned up but already all swollen, was limping around gingerly, cleaning up the bloody mess my father's insanity had left behind.

Just another day in paradise.

My father would beat my mother because he would recall that he saw her smiling for what was—in his mind—an inappropriate amount of time at a customer from the gas station. Or that someone else had smiled at her. It was always something petty like that. He would come home, barge through the door, find his way to her, and beat her in the same venomous manner over and over again. And again, it was always Aunt Helena to the rescue.

Once my mother got a beating because, in Caesar's eyes, she'd risked my life in allowing me to go for a weekend visit with Aunt Helena, her daughter Ana, and Jan, a friend of Helena's. The problem wasn't the visit itself, but rather the state I returned in, as it wasn't the best of trips.

The mountains and countryside of Slovakia are a delight to visit—very scenic and fun to drive through. Ana and I were always eager when the time came to go for a visit at family friends' houses in the country. For me, it was mainly an escape from the hell of witnessing my parents' fights, so I was happy to go just about anywhere at any time.

For this trip, I remember being in the back seat of an old gray car, a Skoda. I was behind another passenger, Havel, Ana sat beside me in the middle, and Helena sat behind Jan, who was driving. Of course, no one wore seatbelts and children's car seats were not in use yet. We were like ping pong balls in a glass jar.

We drove for over an hour through small villages surrounded by lush green forests. The villages all had square, peach-colored stucco houses with gardens in front of each one, chickens running around freely here and there and tiny white churches breaking up the domestic spread. Throughout the drive, Jan and Havel would repetitively pass each other a bottle of Slivovica, a homemade alcohol made from prunes. They got drunk very quickly.

We were just about to cross a small cement bridge in one of those tiny villages when Jan called out in a light-hearted, conspiring tone, "Hey, do you see that beautiful woman there? Let's scare her!" Without further warning, he turned the steering wheel toward the woman and floored the gas pedal. The poor woman leapt to the side just in time, our car missing her by seconds.

Instead of slamming into her, we crashed into the cement bridge with full force. Havel went flying through the window, ending up on the bridge with his eyeballs hanging out of his sockets. Helena had time to shelter Ana with her arm, shoving her to the floor and likely saving her life. However, she couldn't reach me, and my head slammed into the window, the skin of my forehead splitting open from my hairline down to my eyebrows. In shock, I felt the warm blood streaming down into my eyes and onto my cheek and neck. I looked down and saw the stream of red on my shirt.

Villagers arrived from every direction. One of them must have taken me out of the car—I don't really remember who it was or how he did it. All I remember is waking up in a tiny kitchen in one of the villagers' houses, being held down by multiple pairs of hands. A younger woman was standing in front of me telling me that everything would be okay, but that she had to stich my forehead because it was bleeding profusely and that going to a hospital was not an option—we were much too far from one.

I remember staring at her, frozen by fear.

She took up a sewing needle, threaded it, and burned the tip of the needle with a candle in order to disinfect it. She slowly approached my swollen, bleeding forehead, as if she wasn't quite sure of what she was doing. She gave a signal to the man standing behind me who was holding my head, and he poured Slivovica on the gash. It stung and burned, but I still couldn't seem to react.

The woman stuck the needle into my delicate skin. One stich after another, I endured the agonizing pain. It was like I was in another universe. I knew what was going

25

on, I felt the pain, but I just couldn't move; not only because of the five men holding me down, but perhaps also because I was still in shock.

At some point I heard screams coming from close by. "Hey, listen you!" a voice called out. "There is a child in the kitchen next door whom we haven't heard a peep from, and here you are yelling and crying like a baby? Let me put your eyes back in and wash you up. And for crying out loud, stop yelling!" This was obviously directed at the still-drunk Havel, who was clearly in agony.

The woman finished her last stitch, poured additional Slivovica on top of the wound, and patted me on the belly, letting me know that I'd done really well and that she was proud of me. One of the men lifted me up from the kitchen table and softly laid me down in one of the more comfortable chairs close to the wall at the end of the kitchen room. I waited there in my zombie-like state amongst the commotion of the blabbering villagers who'd gathered in the tiny house. They all seemed to look at me with sympathy. I sat and waited until someone—I don't remember who—picked me up and placed me in a car.

We drove back to Hnusta—no seatbelts this time, either—where my mother promptly got into a lot of trouble with Caesar, who blamed her for his daughter's disfigured head.

The physical violence I witnessed wasn't limited to just to our family. A few months after the accident, while running to get Aunt Helena in the hopes of her stopping yet another of my mother's beatings, I saw something that will forever be embedded in my brain, like a gruesome horror movie playing over and over behind your eyelids that just won't go away. I was racing downstairs from our apartment when suddenly I lurched to a stop on the lower floor, frozen by the scene unfolding before me.

The door of the apartment one floor below ours was open. In front of that door was a man grappling with a woman desperately trying to free herself. Later, I was told it was his wife, and that she had had an affair. His bent arm was around her neck and they were leaning backwards, the back of her head on his chest. In his right hand was an old-fashioned straight razor—the kind people call a cutthroat razor. As I watched, he slashed his wife's throat from left to right three times. Right away blood started gushing from the poor woman's wounds as she collapsed to the floor, scrabbling at her ruined neck. I will never forget her eyes when she saw me, nor the screams. I didn't understand what was going on. I saw pure rage in this man's eyes, and I was completely paralyzed with fear.

"I cut her...I cut her...I cut her..." he kept repeating over and over.

After what seemed an eternity, I came to my senses enough to continue on to Aunt Helena's—regardless of what I had just witnessed, I still needed to get her to come with me back to our apartment to help my mother.

The man had not even seen me in his enraged state of mind—or he had and just didn't care. Aunt Helena, hearing the commotion, came running from the floor below before I could reach her apartment. She was the one who took the razor from the man's hand.

After that experience I stopped talking for nearly a year. When I did eventually start talking again I stuttered for a few more years to come, and to this day, when I get nervous or tired, I find myself stuttering a bit. I guess there are some things that are too traumatic for a young child to see, and one's mind goes into survival mode. There were many nights up through my early teenage years where I would wake up screaming and discover that I'd wet myself in terror.

Final Straw

One day, my mother decided that she'd finally had enough. Everyone knew of my parents' passionate, violent relationship and knew that my mother always went back to Caesar no matter what anyone said. However, one day, one of my father's coworkers snitched on him in an attempt to help my poor mother rid herself of his spell over her. He told my mother that Caesar was with a woman in one of the cottages where he worked. She arrived at the cottage up in the beautiful green mountains, where a curtainless window provided all the proof she needed to see of his infidelity.

Crushed, she went back to the apartment. She'd finally seen with her own eyes what others had been telling her for so long. Out of pure desperation, unable to cope with the grim reality of her life anymore, she swallowed a large handful of pills.

She awoke an unknown amount of time later to a nurse asking her if she was all right. She was in a hospital. My father had found her on the floor of our apartment after he'd come home and decided to take her in.

"Mrs. Laskova," came a voice from the other side of the hospital room. It was a worried customer from the gas station who'd come to check on her. It was a small village and everyone knew about everyone else's business, and he was genuinely concerned for her. "Out of everyone in this world, I never thought I would find you here! Why would you do something like this? You are such a beautiful woman. Let him do whatever he wants to, he's not worth it. He's not worthy of you."

When she came back from the hospital, it took a while for her to get back on her feet. Thinking her life was over, that there would be no one else for her, and that he was all that mattered in the world, she hid in the living room for weeks. Right after work she would just sit on the couch, cringing away from the world, makeup-less and unwashed, hiding from the world as my father continued to cheat openly.

"Let's go for coffee, my dear," Helena suggested one day, tired of watching her friend disintegrating right before her eyes.

"No, I don't want to go anywhere. I don't want to see anybody. I just want to stay here on my couch," was my mother's answer.

"Come here to the mirror—come and see what you look like," Helena pressed. "Come and see what you are doing to yourself for this asshole! And for what? For a whoremonger who fucks everything that moves? Shit on his head and pull yourself together!"

Helena was never one to mince words.

She dragged my mother up by the arm, washed her face, dressed her, put makeup on her, and forced her out the door. She took her to a party in Tisovec, a town about ten minutes away.

Inside the small village tavern was a gorgeous young soldier who was visiting his parents at the time. Every girl in the place was fluttering her eyelashes at him, but he only had eyes for my mother.

The young soldier's attentions proved fruitful thanks to Helena, who noticed his interest and promptly shoved my mother toward him. They hit it off and ended up talking the whole evening, my mother telling him about her situation. That was the beginning of the turning point for my mother where my father's spell over her was concerned. While talking with the soldier, she suddenly realized that destroying her life over a man who didn't respect or really care for her at all wasn't worth it. They spoke until the tavern closed. They exchanged information and said their goodbyes, promising to become pen pals to see where it might lead.

This young soldier's weekly letters strengthened my mother further, but his affections would soon be smothered by my father's evil nature. Caesar, realizing that my mother might move on with her life without him at any moment, tried his luck at getting her back. He knew of my mother's passion for him, knew that he used to be like a God to her, and he used this to his advantage to keep her close.

He began to act more kindly toward her while appealing to her mothering instinct to keep the family together. She succumbed to his wishes, but also told him that if he laid his hands on her one more time, she would file for divorce without notifying him. She wrote to the soldier, letting him know that she was going to give life with Caesar one last try. The soldier warned her that her husband would always be a wife-beater, and, of course, he was right.

It only took two months for the young soldier's words to ring true. One day, my mother saw Caesar in a patisserie around the corner from the gas station having a piece of cake with one of his "whores." He never took us there—his own family—but was perfectly happy to entertain one of his women in plain sight in this way.

The last straw for my mother came one weekend while visiting some friends. My mother ended up playing outside with all the kids, including me. My father—likely only in his twisted mind—saw someone putting his arm around her neck, which infuriated him. He held back until after we came home and had all gone to bed with no idea that anything was the matter. We were awakened by my father's fists. He struck my mother and dragged her to the floor, continuing his insanity by brutally kicking her wherever he could reach.

Aunt Helena to the rescue once more.

My mother did as she had promised months before and went to file the divorce papers the next morning, bruised and battered.

Divorcing during this time in Communist Slovakia was nothing short of a miracle. The practice was frowned upon, and furthermore you needed to be living apart for a year to even have your case considered. But where could a woman live when the government gave the husband an apartment after his studies and army duties, not the wife? If she couldn't go back to living with her family, there was nowhere to go. Many battered women stayed in their predicaments, living in constant fear because of this.

"What is this?" my father asked her in renewed fury when he received the divorce papers a couple of days later.

"You know how to read, so read it. I've had enough. I don't love you anymore and I want a divorce. I was stupid to want to die for someone like you. I'm done!"

"But you know that I'll just lie in court. You know that, right? I will put everything on you," he replied, sneering at her.

"Yes, and you can do and say whatever you want. I don't care anymore. We will see whom the judge believes," she shot back.

When the court date arrived, my mother needed to answer to the judge's tough questions.

"You are aware, Mrs. Laskova, that you have to live separately from your spouse for a year in order to have a divorce," the judge said.

"Yes, I am aware, but where am I supposed to go? My parents are so strict; I cannot endure their constant badgering about why I got married in the first place. I cannot stay with them. I am begging you, please, grant me this divorce."

"Mrs. Laskova, I'm sorry but it cannot be done."

"Please, Your Honor. Please give me a divorce," she pleaded.

"Maybe you can find it in your heart to love him again since you were patient for so long?" the judge asked.

"Your Honor, he's cheated on me for years, he beats me, and I simply cannot take it anymore. I can't even stand to look at him. Believe me when I say that if I was on a deserted island with no one for company but a monkey and him, I would rather be with the monkey. I've had enough!" The judge burst out laughing at this last impassioned statement from my mother, and he regarded her in silence for long, agonizing moments.

"I can see now that you really want that divorce, Mrs. Laskova," he said at last. "And so, I shall give it to you."

Relief flooded through my mother in a wave. A miracle had occurred. Whether it was because she had made him laugh or some other reason, the judge had decided to grant my mother's most fervent wish.

"I don't love you anymore, Caesar. I'm really leaving you," my mother said to my father once they'd left the courtroom.

"We will see. I'll break you for this," he replied.

"No, you cannot break me because I don't love you anymore, don't you see? It's over. You were everything to me, but now I see that you are nothing."

"We'll see," he said once more, smirking at her as he left.

My mother tried going back to her parents' house after the divorce, but living with the constant pestering from her father—*I told you so...you didn't listen to me when you wanted to marry that monster, but you did it anyway...you put yourself in this predicament*—proved to be too much to take. She went back to the apartment in Hnusta, clinging to what pride she could in not letting Caesar keep all of her furniture and other belongings for himself, not to mention an apartment where he now enjoyed the freedom to do whatever—and whomever—he wanted.

My wish to live with my mother after the divorce was granted, and I lived with her in the bedroom at the end of the living room—Caesar had taken my room. He and my mother struck a deal in which they would live as roommates as the apartment was close to both of their jobs, my mother didn't want to go back living with her nagging parents, and the impossible task of getting an apartment as a single woman prevented us from living on our own. They agreed not to bring any lovers into the apartment; an agreement that he broke repeatedly as he continued to "entertain" woman after woman.

He was supposed to pay monthly alimony, which he somehow managed to get out of quite often. One day I asked him for 10 Koruna—I don't remember for what exactly, gum perhaps, and he barked at me and sent me across the street to get it from my mother instead. She was working at the gas station during the day and the bakery at night, getting only three hours of sleep so that we could pay for rent and mediocre groceries, which he also didn't help much with. He had his side of the fridge and we had ours—a habit that stayed with him for the rest of his life.

My father was quite unhappy when my mother came back to the apartment, as her presence abolished his sense of freedom and autonomy post-divorce. Predictably, the beatings began anew.

One Sunday afternoon, I needed a pen to do my homework. I asked my mother for one and she told me to ask my father since she was busy with cooking and laundry and didn't have time to find one for me. I went to see my father and promptly froze at the scene before me. My father and *Zubachka*, one of his many "lady" friends—we called her *Zubachka* because of her big teeth, which is what the word means—were in the middle of having sex. I rapidly left and went back to tell my mother.

"Mami...they were naked...and you know...what they were doing...you know..." I stuttered shyly.

By the time my father emerged to get a glass of water, my mother was livid.

"Listen, don't you know how to behave? Do you have to bring your whores to the house? We had an agreement about not bringing anyone here, and you're breaking it.

Can you at least not bring your whores to the apartment when our child is here?"

"Don't insult my girlfriend!" he shouted, smacking her face so hard that she flew across the kitchen table. She hit her head on the floor and her nose started to bleed profusely.

When she got up, she decided to make a visit to his bedroom to give *Zubachka* a piece of her mind.

"Listen here, how can you be with such an ignorant person? Who hits his ex-wife? What, do you think that he loves you? Do you have any pride in yourself at all? Do you think that he only has you? He cheated on me through our whole marriage, and he will cheat on you. You think you are unique and special?" *Zubachka* just laid there on my bed, naked, playing with her necklace in her mouth and smirking at my mother as she railed.

Caesar didn't retaliate against my mother after her rant, instead leaving her with only a bleeding nose—a rare mercy.

Shortly after this incident, my mother was looking for meat in the fridge—meat was still scarce at the time, but we had gotten our hands on some—and she couldn't find it anywhere. While she was searching she noticed my father slouching in the chair beside the kitchen table with an amused look on his face.

"Hey, if you're looking for the meat, it's gone. We ate it. My girlfriend and me."

My mother wheeled on him. "You bastard! For me, I don't care, but gorging on your own child's food! And on top of it, you're laughing about it? You don't even give your child money for candy!" He just kept grinning at her, clearly enjoying her rage and frustration.

When my uncle Lubo came to visit my mother one day at the apartment, Lubo wanted to have a drink.

"I would give you some, but I don't have anything," Caesar told him.

"But you do. You have a homemade bottle up in the cupboard," my mother replied, thinking that he had forgotten about the bottle and that she was helping him.

Once Lubo had left, my father broke my mother's jaw. In his mind, she'd undermined him in front of company. She sustained permanent damage to her eye and jaw from that beating. He apologized the next day, but little good would it do her.

My mother, civilized as she was and still is, even made coffee for Caesar's girlfriends from time to time. By this point she'd moved beyond jealousy, which enraged my father even more. He continued to antagonize her at every turn. Out of the blue, he would try to trip her by sticking his foot in front of her when she was passing by. My mother had long since learned this trick, however, and would just skip over his foot.

One day, my father kicked her in her behind as she was passing by the living room out of pure spite. My mother hated when he "kicked her in the ass" even more than she hated getting beaten up, and she reacted by picking up the tall vase in the living room, intending to smash it over my father's head when he wasn't looking. Just as she was about to send it crashing down, Helena arrived and grabbed the vase from her shaking but determined hands.

"What, you're defending *him?*" my mother yelled.

"Are you crazy? Are you stupid?" Helena yelled back at her. "Do you want to go to jail because of this asshole?" Still infuriated, my mother reluctantly heeded Helena's warning and put down the vase.

Although my mother had moved on from her feelings of jealousy about my father bringing women home, my father would throw fits if she did the same. A couple of days after the ass-kicking incident, my mother went out with Helena and met a tall, handsome man named John. She invited him over for coffee with Helena and two other friends of hers. My father wasted no time in displaying his displeasure with this development.

"Why are you bringing assholes here?" he yelled at her once the guests had gone, slapping her across the face.

"Oh, so it's okay for you to bring your bitches here for years, screwing them in front of your child, but it's not okay for me to have people over?" she snapped back. He backed down from this particular confrontation, but retaliated a few weeks later when she was getting ready to go out with her friends. Apparently enraged by the sight of my mother moving on with her life, he decided to viciously punch her so hard across the face that he broke one of her front teeth. Because she wasn't going to give him the satisfaction of ruining her evening, she stuck the busted tooth back on with a piece of gum. I just sat there in silence as this scene played out, hoping nothing more would come out of it.

My father's frequent beatings left behind a path of destruction on my mother's body for the rest of her life. The foot and ankle he twisted still hurt her. One of her eyes just starts to water out of the blue when she gets tired. Her wrist and arm get sore when she moves a certain way. Her jaw cannot open at times and gets locked up. But mostly, it's her head. She frequently endures headaches, dizziness, pain, throbbing, and a general sense of mental heaviness from all the blows and falls she sustained in her years with my father.

So why the hell did she stay? I must admit that, here in the West, it's easier to judge a battered woman for staying when many have access to women's shelters, legal help, financial assistance, and more. But only a battered woman can understand why she stays with the monster that abuses her. There are more options for women here in the West, but whether in present-day North America or the Slovakia of my childhood, it's the psychological conditioning, the complicated element of having children in the home, and the ever-tempting "I'm sorry" the next day that probably make women stay.

In my mother's case, it was also living under Communism that kept her in her situation. My father held a very prestigious position in the village and he had many connections in the police department, which he happily took advantage of. My mother couldn't get a place of her own. And so we stayed, even though things were just as bad if not worse than they were before the divorce.

Seeds of Escape

A couple of months before the escape, my mother and some of her friends went to a tavern where Caesar played the clarinet with other musicians. He saw her flirting with another man, which enraged him as usual, but he didn't show his rage until my mother went to sleep later that night.

She awoke to punches.

He grabbed her by her long, beautiful hair with one of his powerful hands, dropped her on the floor—twisting her ankle in the process—and continued to punch her repeatedly, breaking her nose. Blood splattered all over his aqua blue shirt, the floor, and the walls. Every time she tried to get up she fell again, her ankle not able to bear her weight and the force of my father's punches and his grip on her hair unrelenting.

"Please, my dear Caesar, please let me go! I'm covered in blood; just let me go wash myself up in the bathroom," she pleaded, hoping he would release her long enough to get away from him for even a second.

By some miracle, he listened to her pleas. She made her way to the bathroom, turned the tap on, and undressed. I don't know why she didn't try to flee the apartment then and there—perhaps she was in shock. The bathtub rapidly filled up with pink-tinted water as she leaned over the tub, bleeding.

Little did my mother know that, in this brief moment of reprieve, my father was gearing up for a renewed attack. Suddenly he barged in the bathroom, fists flying again, catching my mother unaware.

She fell into the tub with the force of his blows, and water splattered everywhere. He shoved the palm of his hand over her mouth and bloody nose in an attempt to drown her. She tried to fight back, pushing at his hands only for him to decide to change his tactic. He seized her neck with both of his hands, squeezing tighter and tighter beneath the reddish water. She tried to grab ahold of the tub's edges for leverage, but our tub had sharp, jutting sections of exposed metal on its sides, and her fingers were sliced to pieces as she fought to fend off my father's renewed attack. The more she tried to free herself from his hold by pulling upward, the further he pushed her under.

Petrified, breathless, and fearing that she was near death, what she did next saved her life: she played dead. She willed herself to stop fighting back, went limp, and waited for an opportunity to get out of the water, which she got when he removed his hands from her neck, trusting that he had succeeded in drowning her.

Once his hands were gone from her neck, she sat up in the tub swiftly and braced herself in a more stable position. "Please calm down, please, please!" she frantically pleaded to my father, who immediately tried pushing her back down into the tub, but this time she had such a good grip that he couldn't manage it.

Exasperated with his failed attempt, he sprinted out of the bathroom to the kitchen—perhaps to get a knife—leaving my mother a small opening for escape. She took this opportunity to quickly get out of the tub and, still naked, started to run as fast as she could, sprained ankle and all, for the front door of the apartment. Thankfully, it was unlocked.

She pounded on every door, crying out for help, but no one took her in—they had all heard her screams before and assumed that she and Caesar were just having another one of their crazy fights. With my father closing in, two stories below a door finally opened and a lady grabbed her by the hand, pulling her inside.

The woman who'd grabbed my mother was employed by the government to wash the floors of the building, and had been given an apartment in return. Seeing my mother covered in blood and bruises, her face swollen and disfigured, fingers bleeding, she told her that she had had enough of watching her get into this state over and over again and that she needed to do something about it. While the lady clothed and washed her, she told her that she needed to lay charges against my father because she might not encounter another kind soul who would help her like this the next time he beat her within an inch of her life.

My mother, now clean and dry, recovered at the tenacious little woman's apartment for about an hour and then went to the police station to finally bring charges against Caesar.

"Mrs. Laskova, finally!" one of the chiefs said when she arrived and told them why she was there. "It's about time. We all know how much you have suffered and for so many years. I am happy to see you here, finally doing something about it." He was the only one not afraid of my father since he would soon be retiring. The rest of the police officers were all either afraid of Caesar or were used to favors from him for special treatment; hence they kept quiet and did nothing when they saw my mother's bruises at the gas station.

My mother found it difficult to come right out and say what my father had done to her. "He just got crazy...he didn't know what he was doing. I am sure he is sorry about it now," she said to the chief, who didn't relent.

"Believe me, Mrs. Laskova, he knew exactly what he was doing. I can guarantee you that when we go to the apartment, he will be cleaning up the mess to conceal the evidence."

Sure enough, when they arrived in the apartment a few hours later, Caesar was in the washroom, cleaning up the bloody walls and scrubbing at his blood-stained aqua shirt.

My mother stayed with the woman downstairs who had taken her in that night, but the next day she had to go back.

"Please forgive me...please forgive me...I am so sorry...please withdraw your complaint," my father begged when he saw her.

"Absolutely not! This time, no way. You beat me and try to kill me? Absolutely not," she replied with determination. Finally defeated, he let the subject go. The next morning, she went to work as usual at the gas station, covered from head to toe in bruises. She received a visit from one of the police officers that day—a friend of Caesar's.

"Mrs. Laskova, please withdraw your complaint," the officer said, clearly trying to intimidate her with his presence. "You know, he is a very important person here...he is an engineer, after all."

"No! He beat me constantly for so many years, and now he continues even though we are divorced. He brings his whores to the house, he neglects his daughter...No!"

It was this move that ultimately triggered my father's plot of revenge to get her back in the worst possible way. He knew he was finished and that very soon he would have to face the consequences of his actions and serve jail time. He started to amass money by asking my mother if she would pay for his share of the rent for two months. Naïve as she sometimes was, my mother didn't ask questions, and this gave him the chance to accumulate enough money for his escape plan without having to tell a single soul.

My father and I were not very close. He didn't really love me; well, at least I didn't ever feel love from him. Ours was far from a beautiful relationship between a father and a daughter.

I remember just a couple of foggy memories of time spent with him in those troublesome times. He would every now and then put me on his shoulders for his exercise routines in the mornings up on the hill at the outskirts of the village. Once, he threw me into deep water and left me behind in the hopes of me learning how to swim on my own. I nearly drowned. I remember getting lost one day on a beach in Bulgaria, and instead of taking me in his arms and comforting me, he followed me from afar to see what I would do, watching my every distressed move as I asked random strangers if they'd seen my "mommy" while crying profusely. He eventually came to get me and promptly smacked me on my behind for getting lost in the first place. I was six.

He did not take me away from my mother out of love for me, but rather out of spite toward her—something he eventually admitted to my mother later on in Greece.

Meanwhile, In Greece

We arrived in Athens, Greece late in the summer of 1981. The immigration office placed us in a very simple hotel called Arcadia right away, where all the immigrants stayed. It was below the majestic Acropolis in the heart of an earsplitting city with millions of people, which was quite overwhelming when you'd just arrived from a little village called Hnusta.

We lived in that hotel for six months.

Canada was Caesar's first choice of country because at that time it had the shortest waiting period to obtain the necessary papers for legal immigrant status. While we waited, he got a job in the Coca Cola factory in Athens. He went to work every day and left me by myself in the hotel. At the age of eight, I fended completely for myself.

He gave me some money from time to time so that I could buy myself souvlaki pita at the corner street vendor. I would wander the busy, noisy streets of downtown

Athens alone every day. I was surrounded by strangers, and I'd never seen so many people in my short life. It was quite overwhelming. As you might imagine, a young girl left alone in a big city was a recipe for disaster.

"Your father wants to see you upstairs in the room. Come with me, and I'll take you to him. He asked me to get you," a familiar man whom I'd seen somewhere around the hotel said to me in a kind voice one day as I was wandering. I was so naïve and trusting at that age, and I followed him to his room. He opened the door, I walked in, and right away he closed the door and locked it. I didn't think anything of it at the time.

Then he picked me up like I was a sack of potatoes and tossed me on top of the bed. He got on top of me and sat on my little chest up near my mouth, trapping my arms between his legs. He unzipped his pants, took out his erect penis, and tried to shove it inside my mouth while grunting with a sense of urgency words beyond my vocabulary. The one thing I'll always remember from the terrifying encounter was the disgusting smell of his penis, like he hadn't washed in months. I was shocked, paralyzed.

I must have had an angel close by looking after me that day, because while he was desperately trying to shove his penis in my mouth, getting more and more aggravated by the second because I had my mouth clamped tightly shut, there was a knock at the door. Insanely frustrated, he got off me and went to the door. When he opened it, I jumped up and shot out of the room like a torpedo. I ran to the washroom at the end of the hall, hoping to hide there temporarily—unfortunately for me, it was a men's washroom.

As if I hadn't been through enough already that day, a blond Romanian in his late twenties looked at me while he finished his business and then started to walk toward me. When he got to me, he quickly shoved me against the wall while his hand made its way into my panties.

He started to fondle me with his finger in the entrance of my vagina, smelling his hands afterwards and licking them while smiling at me with an ugly smirk. He did not rape me, but it felt like he did anyway.

Somehow, I managed to get out of there. I think I was just a game for him. I just didn't understand why was this happening to me, or where the hell my father was. Wasn't he supposed to protect me?

From that day on, I tried to stay close to the people I "trusted"—as much as I could trust anyone in our new life. It took me two weeks to tell my father about that incident; I was ashamed and felt like I'd done something wrong, and I was still plagued by visions of my father beating up my mother. I did tell him eventually, but I don't remember if he did anything about it. All I know is that it didn't happen again. Well, not in Greece, anyway.

My Mother's Unanswered Cries

While I was living through my ordeals in Greece, my poor mother was desperately doing everything in her power to try to get me back. In Communist Slovakia, there was next to nothing she could do.

She tried the Red Cross, explaining that her ex-husband had kidnapped her daughter and escaped through Yugoslavia. She told them that the KGB had come to see her about it, but that they wouldn't help get me back. She showed them the papers proving that I really was her daughter and begged them to help her get a visa to go to Greece, where she knew I was.

"We're so sorry, but we can't do anything as we have no jurisdiction in that country," they told her. Disappointed but not deterred, she tried to get a visa on her own in order to travel to Yugoslavia in the hopes of finding me. Unfortunately, at the time every citizen could only apply for a visa once every five years, in January. In order to get the visa, she first needed permission from the passport office, from her employer, and from the bank, which for various reasons wasn't possible for my mother. She tried anyway. Her application was predictably rejected, and she couldn't try again for the next five years.

While she was waiting for any type of opportunity to show itself, she decided to write to the presidential office, even though the letter would probably never be read. All her friends told her that she was crazy to write to the president, fearing that she would be thrown in jail.

"Well, what of it?" my mother said to her friends. "I am not writing them stupidities, and I've done nothing wrong. They claim to their own citizens and to the whole world that we are free. They write everywhere in the newspapers and on TV that we are a democracy!" The government was indeed declaring to the whole world that we were a democracy—that the people were free and that there was no communism, which was a pure lie, of course.

With this in mind, she bravely penned her letter. In it, she addressed the president directly, saying, "You declare to the whole world that we are a democracy, so why am I not able to get a visa to get my daughter back from Greece, where my ex-husband has taken her without my consent? I have all of my divorce documents proving that the courts gave me sole custody of her. I have provided you with said documents in this letter. I am not asking for money—I will use my own, what little I have. Why can't I go and bring my daughter back home? Please, I need your help."

The presidential office replied. It was hardly more than a note saying that there was nothing they could do.

"Well, no Red Cross, no presidential office...no one wants to help!" my mother said to my sister and her closest friends when the letter came. "But I say that if you help yourself, God will help you. I will figure out a way to escape, I promise you that."

"There is no way that you can do it," one of her friends replied. "They will never give you any papers. Never."

"Just watch me. You wait and see," she vowed, more determined than ever.

A couple of weeks later, my mother and Aunt Helena went to a little coffee shop together and met a lady who would read your future in the coffee grinds left behind in your cup.

Sometimes destiny places certain people in your path, giving you that much-needed push in the right direction.

The woman took my mother's empty cup with only grinds remaining, turned the cup upside down, spun it around a few times, looked straight into my mother's green eyes, and announced her discoveries.

"I see here that you are going through a puddle," the woman said, surprise written across her face. At the time, the expression "going through a puddle" meant going across a border—namely, escaping.

"Really?"

"Yes, really! Look here," the woman said, pointing to something in the cup. My mother looked on, bewildered.

"And I see a baby...you see, there is a stork here." The woman gestured again to the inside of the cup. "Do you have a baby over the puddle?"

"Yes, yes I do," my mother replied, her heart in her throat.

"I see that you will go very, very far over the puddle, and that you will succeed!" the woman finished, a smile on her face.

My mother was delighted. She left the coffee shop that day with a heart bursting with hope.

This mystical encounter paved the road toward my mother's eventual success in her attempts to get me back—a hard-won success that would take five years to plan and execute. My mother took her destiny into her own hands that day, even though it took years for that destiny to manifest.

Proof of Life

"Mrs. Laskova! Mrs. Laskova! I have good news for you! You have a letter. It's from Greece!" the postmaster yelled, holding the letter tightly in her hand as she ran through the streets toward my mother's gas station. Everyone in town knew that "Mr. Engineer" had escaped with his daughter, and they all knew my mother and sympathized with her plight.

Overjoyed, she called Helena to come to the station, and together they opened the letter. Inside, there was a picture of me and a tape recording of my voice. I remember talking to her into the machine as it recorded, saying, "Hi Mami, we are here in Greece but we are going to some kind of stupid Canada, and I don't want to go there but Caesar said that we have to. I told him that I want to go home, that I don't want to go there, but he said that we *had* to go. So I will go to stupid Canada, but I will come back very soon. I will wrap myself in a little package and I will send myself back home!"

At the time, I had no idea who or what Canada was—my father told me next to nothing about our plans. Little did I know that Canada was a place that I would eventually call home; a place I would one day consider myself fortunate to have found.

While my mother was overjoyed to have physical proof that I was alive and well—albeit far away—this news came at a sad time for my family. Both my poor grandfather and my father's father died before I had even left Greece for Canada. I believe that both of them died because of my father's cruel act of taking me away from my family in Slovakia. Their hearts couldn't take it anymore when the KGB confirmed that my father had in fact kidnapped me.

My mother visited her father in the hospital before he passed; he'd caught a cold, and since he had leukemia, the cold was much more threatening than it would normally have been. He was in a bad way. My grandmother told him, "Celinka is coming," and the poor man thought she was talking about me, as my mother and I have the same first name. He opened his eyes for a brief moment in his haziness, only for his hopes to be crushed when he realized they were talking about my mother, not me.

When my grandmother came back that afternoon, there was a mattress tipped up against the window of his hospital room—a sign letting her know that he had died.

A few months later, a long-awaited phone call came from my father one evening at my grandmother's house.

We were just about to leave for Canada. It had been nearly six months since we'd arrived in Greece. My father coolly informed my mother that we were in Greece, and that the tickets to Canada had already been arranged.

"You bastard, you son of a bitch!" my mother seethed. "You kidnapped our daughter, you killed my father, you killed *your* father...You pig! So that's why you call now, because you have your ticket in hand and no one can get to you? What have you done, Caesar?"

"I wanted to take revenge on you, of course," he replied, enjoying her distress.

"Revenge? For what? For whom? Even your own father, whom you basically sentenced to death by grief because you've stolen his granddaughter? Is this how you repay him? Because he raised you well, because you have a degree and an amazing job because of him? Is this how you repay your mother's love, too? Are you not ashamed?"

My great-grandmother, standing next to my hysterical mother while she ranted into the receiver, attempted to reason with her.

"Don't talk to him like that, he will hang up on you and you will never know anything more! You have to talk to him nicely." She took the receiver from my mother's trembling hands.

"Caesar, my dear, where are you, my dear son? You know how much we always loved you," she told him in an even, soft tone, even though all of them despised him with good reason. For me, she would put her hatred aside in order to try to get some type of information from my father. But it was in vain—he divulged nothing useful, only repeating the same information he'd already told my mother, and then he hung up the phone.

After this glimmer of hope, my mother was left in darkness for the next seven years—years that would ultimately shape me into the complex human being that I am now.

Montreal, 1982 - 1988

Our six-month sojourn was coming to an end in the land of the gods. My time with my father traveling around Greece resulted in some abnormally fond memories. Despite the circumstances, I have vivid recollections of exciting adventures that I've grown to love and for which I still yearn. A new era was born within me alongside this new sense of appreciation for living life on the edge.

I remember on one of those adventurous days we stole large, delicious watermelons from the fields overlooking the crystal-clear aquamarine waters of the Mediterranean Sea, running away in a rush in the hopes of not getting caught. We brought them down to the magnificent beach with us, where we let them cool in the crisp sea water and devoured them like mad dogs once they were chilled.

Sometimes we would jump from enormous, rocky cliffs into the uncertainty of the sea below, where the margin of error was very small and one mistake could potentially end your life. We hopped on local fishing boats when we went for our lengthy swims, and the fishermen welcomed us onboard with open arms, offering us all kinds of delicious food.

I remember on one of those occasions when the fishermen were hauling in their catch, one of them hurriedly but kindly shoved me to the front of the cabin, saving me from the enormous, creeping octopus that was slowly escaping through the net and making her way onto the deck of the boat. They were able to apprehend the slippery creature, but not without any injuries. One of the fishermen was scarred by the octopus's suction cups and sharp beak as she defended herself in the hopes of being released. Poor creature.

Once the situation had resolved itself, the same fisherman who had shoved me out of the way handed me a tiny seahorse on a string, which I wore proudly. I wore that seahorse for months until it broke.

We visited places like the parliament buildings and the majestic Acropolis overlooking the city, where leftovers of ancient buildings—including the bruised and battered Parthenon and its colonnades—still stand the test of war, earthquakes, and time itself to watch proudly over the city.

The uneasiness of unfamiliar earthquakes shook me inside and out while transitioning into the new me during this time. It was here in the land of the gods that my survival mode kicked into full gear, and my father was becoming my rock, my only family, the only one keeping me alive. Even though he mistreated me, he was becoming my life. The memories of a mother who truly loved me were rapidly becoming a thing of the past, and my love for this man who wouldn't even let me call him Father grew stronger by the day—almost to the point of infatuation. I understood many years down the road why I grew so attached to someone like my father who'd acted so abominably, but back then I only knew that I loved him.

We arrived in Montreal, Quebec late in the evening on New Year's Eve, 1981.

We were extremely well treated and welcomed with open arms in this land of opportunities. We spent our first night in a quite sophisticated room on a higher floor of a decent hotel in downtown Montreal. Looking out the large window, I noticed the brand-new scenery, so different from Greece. There was nothing old here; only huge, elegant buildings, noiseless streets, and what appeared to be a very well-organized city stretching out into the distance. I remember watching an Elvis Presley movie that night as I tried to settle in to our new surroundings.

A couple of days later, they transferred us to our new apartment. I didn't know it at the time, but the small brown bugs with fast legs that we called our "pets" were actually cockroaches. We stayed in this apartment for a few months, and then moved to a nicer apartment with a pool in the complex.

I started to go to school—a French one, of course—and it was quite a challenge for me. Adjusting to a new country, learning a new language, and meeting new people all while having no friends, no mother, and only the company of a man who never had anything nice to say to me and treated me as a distraction at best was extremely difficult.

Homework was an enormous chore—I remember being called "stupid" and, my favorite, my father yelling "Why don't you know this? How can you not see the answer?" Nonetheless, I soon developed a routine and made the best of this new life of mine.

Sometimes history repeated itself in ways that I would have preferred it not to. When I was ten and we were living in our second apartment, I had a gray cat by the name of Minette as my new pet. My father had bought her for me—or he'd gotten her on the street, I'm not really sure—in the hopes of filling the motherless void in my life. Minette, the little Houdini, promptly escaped. I of course went looking for her, calling her name throughout the corridors of the small three-story building which was being revamped.

As I wandered in the construction zone, a man opened a door.

"Are you looking for your cat? Because I think that I saw here in here, but you need to come and get her. She doesn't want to come to me," he said to me politely. Blind, innocent, trusting little me went right along with his ploy. I must have forgotten the previous incident in Greece somehow.

Once I came inside he quickly shut the door and locked it. He shoved me up against the wall, held both of my hands above my head with one of his, and put the other down my pants. He went back and forth from grabbing my chest to grabbing my crotch. I can't recall if it hurt; what I do remember is the horrendous feeling of shame at the thought that I had somehow put myself in this situation once again. I was beside myself with horror—I'd trusted this idiot, this monster that I'd thought was trying to help me. How could I have fallen for this again?

I must have had a higher power watching over me once more, because I somehow freed myself from his grip and run like my life depended on it—in reality, it probably did. I went straight for the door, which I somehow was able to unlock, and ran down to my apartment, locking the door behind me once I was inside. I went to my bedroom, closed the door, and pondered what seemed to me at the time to be my extreme lack of intelligence. I don't know if he ran after me. I just couldn't grasp what had happened.

I told my father a few weeks later, thinking it was my fault for following the man and worried that he would blame me. Although my father did try to find him this time (he was a construction worker, not a resident of our apartment), he was long gone by the time I'd spoken up.

The years spent in my father's company were not a calm walk in the park. Woman after woman would enter our lives, and every time I really liked one of them my father would break up with her and then do it all over again, leaving me heartbroken. I was desperately trying to replace my mother, whom I thought had abandoned me. I was becoming repulsed by it all, and hearing "funny" noises from my father's bedroom all the time didn't help. Once he had used them, he would throw his women out like they were nothing. I remember on several occasions talking to them, trying to make them feel better once he'd ravaged their self-image and esteem—a child comforting an adult as best she could.

My father had become accustomed to telling me how stupid I was for not understanding my homework, and I disclosed less and less and hid more and more. I repeated my grade in school, my father entirely oblivious to the why of the matter.

Despite the constant challenges, I was adjusting to my little life in Canada. Every year during summer break, my father would put me in a Czech summer camp for the whole two months so that he could have his independence and do whatever with whomever he wanted. His friends called him the Montreal Gigolo, after all.

I became a little tomboy—not least because of my father's antics. We would wrestle on many occasions, and he would become overzealous and choke-hold me to the point of nearly breaking my neck. I would shout out with a feeble voice in desperation, demanding for him to let me go.

He enrolled me in karate, a wonderful sport that I wish I had had more desire to participate in at the time, but I didn't have the spirit for it then. Later on when we moved to another city he enrolled me in the air cadets, which I partly enjoyed, but being a little bit of a free-spirited girl, I didn't like people telling me what to do—I had enough of that at home. I think that he meant well, enrolling me in these activities. He was trying in the only way he knew how to teach me ways of defending myself from the monsters who kept entering my life. I think these experiences did make me a stronger person and helped to shape me into who I am today.

When I was about twelve years old, my father and I went to play at the park late on a summer evening. I was swinging away on the swing set, daydreaming, when I was suddenly pushed so hard that I fell down. It was my father, of course. Furious, I screamed "*ti kokot jeden!*"—"you dick!" in Slovak—at him. The expression has much more weight in our language than in English. In response, my father told me not to come home that night, and he left me there all by myself without another word.

But where was I to go? I had nowhere to go *but* home.

After a few hours by myself in the park, night started to descend on the city. I wearily made my way back to our apartment. What a mistake that was. Upon my arrival, my father grabbed me, bent me over his knees, and started to beat me. This would be the only time he would do so, but painful would be an understatement.

One after another, he broke wooden ladles across my fragile back and bum. I was screaming, telling him to let me go, that I was sorry, that I would never do it again, but he continued.

"The more you scream, the more I will hit you!" he said in a familiar tone—it was how he sounded when he was beating my mother. I became extremely frightened at this, and I somehow managed to go to another place in my head. I became quiet.

I don't remember when it all ended; all I know is that when I came back to myself, I was standing on my feet, pantsless. I dragged my aching body, soul, and pride to my room while desperately trying to cover my throbbing behind with the crinkled-up pants from around my ankles.

I was petrified, humiliated, confused, disoriented, and furious—I just wanted somebody to come and take me away. But I knew, or at least I thought I knew, that without him, I would never see my mother again. And so, with my tail between my legs, I vowed to do whatever I needed to in order to survive until my mother could come get me. But I didn't know where she was or why it was taking so long for her to find her way back to me. Did she abandon me? Didn't she want to see me again? These questions plagued me.

As the years passed, there were glimmers of happiness. Every Tuesday we would go for pizza. He took me to museums, different types of concerts, horseback riding, and even on a vacation to Cuba. He had taught me to be tough—really, *really* tough, which is something I carry with me to this day and am grateful to him for in some ways. In time, I would come to understand that what I was feeling toward my father during this period of my life resembled Stockholm syndrome in many ways. In order to survive unpleasant circumstances, you need to still be able to function so as to put one foot in front of the other. He was my father and my captor. I had no other choice but to love him. He was my father, after all, even though I was not allowed to call him that.

More years went by, and life went on—mercifully without any more violent episodes from Caesar. I had survived my pre-teens and now I was a full-blown hormonal teenager at fifteen. We had moved from Montreal to Shawinigan, which is about two hours from Montreal. Shawinigan is a small, cute pulp-and-paper town along the Saint Maurice River, and is home to the beautiful and well-known Shawinigan Falls. My father had secured a position in forestry after redoing part of his education in Canada in order to continue working in the field, which he dearly loved.

Life was as normal as any other teenaged immigrant. I was in high school, and extremely proud of the fact that I had never touched drugs in my life. What I didn't understand at that time was that I was extremely lonely, and my cries for attention were being met by guys who didn't really care for me at all. I just needed some type of attention, some warmth, someone to tell me they loved me, that I was beautiful and worth something. My so-called father certainly wasn't providing any of these things, so, young and alone as I was, I looked elsewhere.

I attached myself to whoever was willing to tell me how gorgeous and special I was. Throughout it all, however, I never succumbed to the allure of drugs. I wanted to have my head clear, and I didn't see what the big deal was in getting high as a kite anyway, especially when I saw a couple of my other "friends" in that state of mind. To this day I have no idea where the strength to say no came from, but I'm grateful for it nonetheless.

My father, keeping true to himself, embarrassed me every chance he got with his indecent proposals to my friends. It got so bad that I didn't want to have any of them over, embarrassed by him as I was—not that I had many friends to begin with. Then again, a few of them enjoyed his games, enamored by my unconventional, handsome father who had a gift for attracting every needy female for miles. Thankfully it never went any further than games.

One thing was certain: my father was a man living in a truly distorted reality.

From Nightmare to Opportunity

*M*y mother never stopped trying to get back to me. She suffered a "mild" heart attack when the KGB told her the dreadful news that my father had taken me. Despite this, and after her failed attempts with the Red Cross and the presidential office, she was more determined than ever to find me. Filled with resolve, she continued on her own destiny's path—a path that would eventually lead back to me.

Once a year, Slovakian citizens had the opportunity to travel within surrounding Communist countries like Hungary, Romania, Poland, and Ukraine. The government allowed this because, as these countries were also under Communist rule, it was just as difficult to escape there as it was in Slovakia. The exception was Poland; being next to the Baltic Sea, a few succeeded by illegally hopping onto tanker ships.

As mentioned previously, once every five years you could apply for a visa to travel to Yugoslavia—with no guarantee of them granting you permission, of course. The reasoning behind the five-year waiting period was to discourage people from forming connections outside of the home country and then using those connections to escape the following year. The government hoped that, after five years, you would get used to the system again and your desire to escape would wane.

My mother was actually on a blacklist that prevented her from obtaining a travel visa to Yugoslavia, as she had family in a capitalist country, including a brother who had escaped a year after my father and I had.

There was no way she could try to leave through Yugoslavia, so she tried her luck through Romania.

Once she arrived in Romania, she quickly realized that there was no way she could escape through the country's borders. Life was harsh in Romania during this time. People had no food—my mother saw people sharing one piece of black, moldy bread and a sheep's head as a meal between themselves—and the Communist leader Nicolae Ceausescu reigned with an iron fist.

She arrived at a simple but very well-protected border in the mountains. She immediately went to see the young soldiers armed with Kalashnikovs, a renowned Russian automatic rifle, guarding the crossing.

"Boys, can you let me through?" she pleaded. "My ex-husband took my daughter and I am trying to get to her. Please, let me through."

"No! Are you crazy? They will shoot us on the spot!" one of the young men replied. "There is no way we can let you pass. I'm sorry, but you have to go back."

She returned to Slovakia and patiently waited another year for her next opportunity.

Once the year had passed, she tried her luck through Bulgaria, since no visas were required to visit. This time she wasn't going to plead with soldiers—she decided to play dumb instead, a choice that could have cost her her life. She offered Josef, her trustworthy coworker from the gas station, a great arrangement. If he would agree to drive her and my sister Maya through the border, she would give him her car in exchange, pending the success of the mission.

The agreement was that Josef, once they had passed the Yugoslavian border, would keep her old yellow Russian moskvich cartoon of a car, and would drive back to Slovakia on his own. Seemingly happy to risk his life for an old car, he agreed. They said their goodbyes to immediate and trusted family members only, signed the transfer documents for the car to Josef, and were on their way.

They arrived at the Bulgarian-Yugoslavian border and were met with booth after booth filled with soldiers— a stark reminder of their lack of freedom. They waited behind a small car, its driver having his documents examined, and as the officer opened the barrier for the car to pass, Josef floored the gas pedal and drove through the gate as it was closing.

What a mistake that was. Huge spikes emerged from the ground a few meters ahead, and Josef slammed on the breaks. Right away, soldiers came running from every corner and every booth, shouting at everyone in the car to get out.

"And where do you think you were going? You want to escape, do you?" they shouted, pointing Kalashnikovs at my mother, Maya, and Josef.

"Please don't shoot us, we thought the gate was opening for us!" my mother cried, trying to play her dumb card. But the guards knew very well what they were up to; my mother wasn't the first, and she wouldn't be the last.

They called the head office in Sofia right away to order a car escort to take them back to Slovakia.

"Please...I am begging you, please cancel the escort! I am just trying to find my daughter! My ex-husband took her and I just want to see her again. Please don't do this!" My mother fell to her knees, knowing that she might be pleading for her life.

In the end, the Bulgarians took pity on my mother and called off the escort, ordering her to return immediately to Slovakia. As they were crossing the Slovak border on their way back, they were all shaking from fear and praying to God that the Bulgarians wouldn't report them to the Slovak authorities. But they were safe. The Bulgarians came through, thank God.

Another defeat! They came back to Slovakia, and my mother changed her plans again. She left her job at the gas station and kept her "new" apartment. Since my father had defected, the government couldn't just throw her out from the apartment that they had shared, so they let her stay there. But it was too big, too expensive, and with it came horrible memories that she couldn't just sweep out the door with the dust. One day an opportunity arose for her to do an exchange with another person who had a smaller place in another building nearby. That person was a coworker of my fathers. It was possible to exchange apartments between people but not to get one of your own at the time.

Leaving Maya in Hnusta with a trustworthy friend (my sister was still going to school there), she then started to tell people that they would soon be moving to Banska Bystrica, 83 kilometers away from Hnusta. She told them that her mother needed help and that she would try to make a brand new life for herself in a new town. This gave her a legitimate excuse to move her furniture and belongings.

Little by little she started to sell her furniture to her cousin in the hopes of saving extra money for her upcoming (and still unplanned) next attempt at escape. She was also now paying less for an apartment, helping her to save even more. She had to be exceedingly careful, as in those times you couldn't sell your belongings to just anyone—few had money to buy them, for one, but mostly because it would attract unwanted attention from too-curious eyes.

While keeping the apartment in case her plot didn't pan out, she started to work in Banska Bystrica. For nearly a year she worked in a variety of different places, unsuccessful in obtaining a visa for Yugoslavia every time she tried. She still needed permission from her employer, the bank, and the passport office in order to get the visa, and she had the added problem of having her name blacklisted because of my father's escape to deal with, as well.

She visited my sister every weekend in Hnusta. They would stay in the empty apartment, catching up on their daily lives and working on possible ways to leave the country. My mother would tell my sister that it was extremely important that she didn't have any friends over to see the mostly empty apartment and that she couldn't tell anyone about their plan to escape.

Five years had passed since my father took me at this point.

My mother decided to try working in a completely different field, where people didn't know of her unfortunate predicament and that she was trying desperately to leave the country. She went to work at a nail and screws manufacturer in a very small village called Tisovec, about 11 kilometers from Hnusta.

Her job involved being given a picture of a huge screw or nail, which she had to then flawlessly and to the millimeter sculpt from iron with a chisel. Duro, the foreman, who liked my mother quite a bit, helped her by stealing screws from others and pretending that the screws were her work, since she had no clue of what she was doing.

In order to give herself time to think and plan, she started to complain about her gallbladder. It was actually hurting her, but she overplayed it immensely in order to get the operation quicker. Most operations in Communist Slovakia were not like they are nowadays. They would cut your belly from left to right, dig in to remove the gallbladder, sew you up, and send you home in extreme pain, where you generally had a month of recovery. But it needed to be done, and it ended up giving my mother the opportunity she was waiting for. She had the painful operation and then stayed at Helena's for a month to recuperate.

This is when the pieces started to all line up at last, setting my mother's final plan in motion.

A few years back, when she was still working at the gas station in Hnusta, fate had brought my mother a gift that she couldn't open until that fated month when she was recovering from her operation. A customer—a short, bald, heavyset gentleman with a kind face and a rather simple mind—had become smitten with her, as many men did. He happened to be the chief of the passport office.

My mother had asked him for his assistance shortly after our escape, but there had been nothing he could do. Time heals all, they say. Time also lets you forget certain details as it passes, and it's possible that the passport chief had forgotten my mother's plea from years ago.

Directly after her one-month recovery, my mother decided to call the man and ask him to get together for a drink, which he immediately agreed to. They went for a drink in a tavern—a typical Slovak abode. The square wooden structure looked more like a house than a bar, and smoke wafted from the chimney in a welcoming way. Inside, the magnificent fireplace hand-crafted with stones made you feel right at home. Meticulously hand-painted ceramic dishes and cups peppered the tabletops, and the stench of beer would stick to you like crazy glue. More than a few would spend their whole evening night after night in taverns like this one across the country, getting good and drunk before heading home.

As they sat down together, my mother started to complain about her gallbladder immediately.

"You know, my gallbladder operation was so painful," she said to her friend, clutching at her stomach. "I think I need to go to the Adriatic Sea in Yugoslavia to heal some more."

"Why don't you go to the Black Sea in Russia?" he asked her, gazing into her beautiful green eyes.

"No, no, absolutely not, I need the Adriatic Sea, not the Black Sea. It heals more than the Black Sea, I've heard," she said with determination. She could tell that he was about to argue the point further, and she pressed on. "The water is a beautiful, clear aqua blue, and it will heal my scars much faster, I know it. Please, will you help me get there?"

He smiled at her, and she knew that she had won him over. "Okay, Celinka. I will help you, but you mustn't leave Yugoslavia, do you hear? You must come back, or I'll be finished for sure."

"What? Of course I'll come back! I am working here at the factory for now, but I will be going back to the gas station soon. I was making more money there—I just need to heal my scars. Of course I won't leave! I love it here. I make good money and life is good." My mother reassured him as best she could, knowing all along that she had to lie to him in order to hang onto any chance of her plan working.

After spending the night with her, the chief of the passport office looked the other way on the matter of my mother's blacklisted name and granted her wish. The rest came easy. The next day she asked Duro the foreman for her second permission slip. He granted it to her gladly.

Once she had these two documents, the bank exchanged some of her money for Yugoslavian Dinar without a hitch—two weeks' worth, no more.

She'd done it.

Final Escape

"Maya, this is it. There is no way I'm coming back, absolutely no way. It took me five years to get the right papers, and I would rather be shot in the mountains trying to escape than to come back. But it's safer for you to stay here in Slovakia. I've told you this already."

"*No*, Mami! They will shoot you, and then they will shoot me! I am going with you. I am not staying here."

My sister was relentless, and my mother eventually gave in.

With the hard-won visa in hand, money, and train tickets, they said their goodbyes to my grandmother, who stayed behind in the village and who had serious doubts about my mother's plans, as she'd already failed two times. In my grandmother's mind, I'm sure that she was certain she would see them again soon.

It was three o'clock in the morning when a friend of the family drove my nervous mother and sister to Filakova, where all the trains departed to surrounding countries.

They boarded a simple, old-fashioned train, and the departure whistle blew. This was it—there was no going back this time. It was do or die, and they were not about to give up. The train's chugging seemed to mirror the rapid beating of their hearts as they slowly disappeared into the darkness of the night and into the unknown.

They transferred trains at the colossal Nyugati station in Budapest, Hungary, built in the 1800s and which looked more like a grand opera hall than a train station, with its massive triangular glass structure hugged by two beautiful church-like structures. Their next train was considerably more elegant, and once aboard they trailed through the planes of Hungary.

My mother was more prepared for this attempt at escape than she'd ever been. She'd sold most of her belongings, accepted what money her mother could give her, and hidden away some illegal American dollars and Dutch marks that she'd gotten from Fero, one of the sons of the chief of police who looked just like the Marlboro man and who knew a thing or two about getting the right stuff from the right people if you were in need of such a thing. All of this amounted to about four hundred U.S. dollars. She hoped it would be enough.

She had to be especially careful with the foreign currency, as it was illegal to have any type of foreign money on you that didn't match your destination—after all, why would you need it unless you were planning to escape? Koruna and Boni were the only currencies that checked out. If by any chance someone overseas sent you foreign money, the bank would automatically change it into Boni, a type of money that could only be used inside the country. It was just a piece of paper with some drawings on it; nothing more, and it was completely useless anywhere else in the world.

My mother knew she had to have a foolproof plan for hiding the cash. She rolled it up and shoved it inside of a tampon, and then wore the tampon inside of her throughout the security check. That's how all the women did it. Knowing that they would soon be interrogated by very skilled officers who knew how to spot a lie, my mother steeled herself and told my sister to stare out the window instead of looking at the officers so that her beautiful face wouldn't reveal anything.

"Papers and visa, please," the SDB control officer said in a cold tone when he approached. My mother handed their papers over. "Do you have any more money than these Dinar?" he asked.

"No, Officer, we don't," my mother replied, trying to remain calm.

"Yes, you do!" he hissed, staring down at her with piercing eyes. She repeated that they did not have any other money, meeting his gaze even though she was shaking inside.

"Okay, so what if we do this—we will stop the train, we go to a gynecologist and he will search you both, and then we will see if you're hiding anything or not."

"You can do that if you wish, but I am telling you the truth. I don't have money. Neither of us do."

He wasn't convinced. "If we do stop the train, do you have any idea how much it will cost you? 50,000 Dinar, that's how much. So tell the truth and just admit that you have the money!"

My mother held her own against the onslaught. "We don't have any money, Officer. I'm sorry, but we just don't."

He continued to glare at her, but gave her back the documents and turned to leave. Just before he disappeared from sight he turned around and said smirked, "Even so...I know you have!" Everyone knew that travelers from where my mother and sister were coming from carried illegal currency with them, and why he let them go, we will never know.

They were that much closer to victory.

They arrived in the seaside town of Split, in current-day Croatia. The train station, a much more modest structure than the one in Budapest, was packed with locals holding cardboard cards advertising much-needed accommodations. They decided to rent from one lady who stood out from the crowd.

They followed the woman they'd chosen by foot through the narrow paths leading out from the train station and soon arrived at her modest little house, where they would stay for the next two weeks. Their room was very rustic, with only a bed and a small table with chairs.

Split was a humble but beautiful holiday destination where many people who lived in Communist countries would come in search of relaxation—and some, of course, came in search of escape. The small port city is surrounded by mountains, and quaint homes and buildings with red clay roofs overlook the gorgeous turquoise-blue waters of the Adriatic Sea. A variety of beaches await the visitors; some rocky, others sandy, and many surrounded by luscious trees. Small shops and restaurants were filled with the pleasing sounds of melodic Yugoslavian songs, creating a jovial atmosphere. It would have surely been a paradise for my mother and sister if they had in fact been visiting for leisure, but this was not their purpose.

The next day, they arrived at UNICEF's headquarters in the town. My mother explained the whole story and told them that they wanted to get to Canada in order to find me. The UNICEF representatives agreed to help them and gave them the application form for political refugees. They filled out the paperwork, not realizing at the time that the fact that Maya's last name was different from my mother's, would create a problem for them down the road.

While they waited for their application to be processed, they weren't going to just sit around. They stayed in their room for a few days and then decided to go to the pier, where ships and ferries came and went to Italy and Greece. Quickly they figured out that there was absolutely no way of getting on one of those ships; they were guarded as if the Queen of England herself were a passenger, and neither my mother's beautiful emerald eyes nor my sister's beauty could charm them onto a ship.

They asked one of the guards securing an Italian ship if he could help them in getting on board, but the least he did for them was not tell the authorities on them. By the time they'd given up on trying to hop a ship, another week had passed. They went back to UNICEF, and were told to come back in another week.

While they were waiting, my sister met an Italian guy and learned some Italian from him. We in the East are notoriously quick learners with languages; it comes to us very easily. This skill would come in handy very soon for my mother and sister.

When they came back to UNICEF after one week with nearly empty pockets and an expired visa, my mother questioned them about the state of their application.

"Why is it taking such a long time? We barely have any money left," she said, worried that something had gone wrong with the application and fearing the worst.

"Why does your daughter have a different last name? Do you have permission from her father for her to go across the border with you?" the UNICEF representative questioned. Maya was only just past sixteen and still considered a child.

"We have been divorced for many years, and the courts awarded me sole custody. My daughter has been with me since her birth, and he is not involved in her life. Why didn't you tell us that there was a problem right away? We've run out of money waiting for you," my mother replied, her frustration and despair mounting.

"Well, that is not our problem. But you absolutely need a letter of consent from her father that she can go with you in order for us to help you," they told her.

It was too late. Clearly, nothing could be accomplished with UNICEF. They'd wasted so much time with their paperwork that she couldn't even go back to Slovakia as her visa had expired.

"Maya, you go back to Slovakia," my mother pleaded with my sister. "They probably won't do much to you, and I am going to try going through the mountains. We won't get another visa for Yugoslavia for another five years, or never, since we didn't come back in time. I'll be finished if I go back."

"No, I am going with you!" my sister insisted.

My mother relented and they stayed together in Split, time and money quickly running out.

━ ━

Slovakia

"Lubo! What did you do?" Lubo's boss demanded when he arrived at work one day.

"What? Nothing! Why?" Lubo replied.

"The KGB was looking for you and wanted to talk to you. What is going on?"

"I don't know," Lubo lied, knowing, of course, exactly what the KGB were after.

At the end of the day, around suppertime, the KGB arrived at my grandmother's door, and Lubo greeted them.

"Mr. Stastny, did you know that your sister has escaped through the border?" they asked.

"No! I didn't know...we know nothing, I swear" he lied.

"Did she write to you?"

"No, we've heard nothing. We know nothing." My mother had been sending them secret letters from Yugoslavia, but he knew better than to tell them that.

"Okay Mr. Stastny, tell me this: did she leave behind any of her property?"

"No, we have nothing of hers," Lubo said.

"Did she leave some gold behind?"

"Gold? From where? We have nothing, I tell you. We are poor."

"Well then. If she gets in touch, we expect you to let us know," one of the agents said as they turned to go.

"Yes, of course we will, right away," Lubo said with a plastered-on smile as he closed the door. "Yeah, for sure I will be calling you to let you know, you sheep!" he whispered to himself through his teeth once it was safe for him to do so.

Not too long after, my grandmother received a letter from the government that informed her that my mother had been sentenced to four years in jail for treason and desertion of the Republic. The letter included a date for my grandmother to make her way to court, where she had to plead that she didn't know anything about her daughter's whereabouts nor her plan to escape. It was an extremely difficult time for escapees' families who were left behind. They were bombarded with never-ending documents and random visits from the KGB, and the evil stares of the Communist regime's supporters stung like daggers.

Once Communism fell in 1989, everyone who had succeeded to escape throughout the regime received amnesty, and it was safe for them to go back to their country without the imminent danger of the KGB arresting them and sending them to jail. It was the beginning of the end for the KGB and ended in 1991. Of course, things were very different while the regime still held power.

— ～

Yugoslavia

Over two weeks had passed, and their stay at the woman's place came to an end. Having nowhere else to sleep, they decided to go to a close by park where gypsies lived like nomads, having nothing else but cardboard boxes to keep themselves warm at night. My mother, determined to survive the bitter cold of the night, decided to steal a cardboard box from one of the gypsies who had left it unattended. In order to be more discreet, they moved under a tree at the outskirts of the park. The stolen cardboard would make the cold dampness of the night a little more bearable. The poor gypsy came to question them about the cardboard box that my mother had taken, and my mother, feeling guilty about her decision to take the man's cardboard but making the decision to put her daughter over this unfortunate soul, told him that she'd found it near the garbage a little further down.

They needed a new plan since the money was vanishing quicker than anticipated. Frustration overcame them both, and soon they had their first fight. My sister had made a Yugoslavian friend during those two weeks named Yuhosh. Exasperated, my mother kept scolding my sister daily because she didn't like her roaming the streets nearly every night with this young man. One day, my sister had enough of being treated like a child and lashed out at my mother.

"Give me money! I want to be alone," she said to my poor mother.

"What money? Tell me, what money, Maya? Did you earn some somewhere that I don't know about? Perhaps you have some hidden money of your own somewhere? You know what, sweetheart, we are going to the train station and I will put you on the train back to Slovakia, to your grandmother's," my mother replied, exasperated.

"No! I am not going back to Slovakia. Just give me my passport and I will go and be alone somewhere," Maya pressed.

"Which passport, Maya? Don't you remember how much trouble we ran into with UNICEF because of your name? We don't have the same last name, so they'll send you back to Slovakia anyway if they find you alone roaming the streets."

Eventually my sister apologized for her behavior, and they put the fight behind them. She was a teenager, after all, and living with a mother whose main purpose in life was to find me must have been extremely difficult for her.

My mother decided to buy a map and study it carefully to see how far Greece was from where they were, since Italy was clearly out of the question. By coincidence my mother met a Serbian woman with short black hair who was all dressed in black with a small black cross tattooed on her hand. Little did my mother know that this woman was a devil disguised as a sweet middle-aged lady. She explained their dire situation to her, and the woman invited them to stay with her for a while—a mistake that could have sent them straight back to Slovakia where severe consequences awaited.

The woman's boyfriend came for a visit not too soon after their arrival at her simple home, and it must have been obvious to him that they were hiding from the authorities. Under their host's watchful stare at the kitchen table, my mother explained their situation to the man, as he seemed amicable and welcoming.

While studying the map carefully in the woman's home, my mother noticed the city of Gevgelia in Macedonia, and decided to take a chance on it. Since Gevgelia is 873 kilometers from Split and only 5 kilometers from the Greek border, it was the perfect town to aim for. She entrusted her suitcase, which was filled with valuable things like the gold she had taken with her from home, to their host and told her that once she was situated in Greece, she would come back for her belongings.

My mother and sister decided to hitchhike the long and dangerous journey as they had no more money, not even for a bus.

Once they positioned themselves on the road, wait-ing for anyone to give them a ride, my mother gave Maya some last-minute instructions.

"Maya, when a car stops, you go and sit behind and I will be in front. In case the driver wants to rape us or kill us, you hit him over the head while I take control of the car. Okay?" My sister nodded, frightened by my mother's words but compliant.

A truck soon stopped and they quickly hopped in. My mother explained their plight to the truck driver, who was going directly to Greece.

"I would take you, but I can't," he said, not unkindly. "When I go through the border, they will check inside the tank and would see you. I can't risk it, I'm sorry. What I can do is leave you just before the border at the motor rest and you can try going through the mountains. If you succeed, then good for you! But if you don't, I will be returning in three days, so wait for me there and I will take you back."

"Okay, thank you. That will be fine," my mother replied.

"Aren't you afraid?" he added with a smile.

"Of what?" she asked him.

"That I might take advantage of you?" he answered with a smirk.

"No. I am not afraid. Why would you rape us? Why would you risk going to prison and die there for something that you can easily get in the city? I don't think you would risk it," she said in as nonchalant a tone as she could.

"You are a fox!" he replied. I don't believe he really wanted to harm them, but rather to make them aware that they were putting themselves into quite a dangerous situation traveling as they were.

By the end of the long drive, the truck driver had developed more sympathy for my mother and sister, and he handed my mother some money.

"Here you go. I can't help you more than that. I hope you will succeed, but I really can't risk it. I hope you understand," he said to her apologetically.

"Of course. Thank you so much," she said, and they hopped out of the truck at the motor rest, which was a kind of a pit stop between borders with picnic tables, a coffee shop, and a money-exchange place where you could either buy something or exchange currency. They bought themselves a coffee with the money that the truck driver gave them and sat at a table. They had to try to fit in and not look too suspicious.

All of sudden, a familiar face emerged through the crowd and headed straight toward them. It was the tattooed woman's boyfriend.

"I knew you would be here," he said, breathing hard. "I left as soon as I found out. Listen, the old brat denounced you, so be careful. She will be on her way here very soon, as well. I don't know how else to help you."

My mother and sister stared at him with their hearts pounding in their chests.

"Damn her!" my mother hissed, trying to focus and think on her feet. "Okay, you can help us by dropping us off at the head of the mountain so that we can try to walk through to the other side." It was a long shot, but my mother believed—at least at the time—that they really could do it.

"Okay," he agreed, and they left as quickly as they dared.

They headed toward the head of a mountain a little bit further from the border, where he dropped them off at the side of the road in the middle of the night. His headlights dimmed and then disappeared as he drove away, and soon they were left in pure blackness.

There was absolutely nothing but pure and utter night. No lights, no fireflies, no moon, not even a shining star. They held each other's hands while slowly creeping forward so as not to trip. They tried feeling around for anything that could guide them, but there was nothing. It felt like they were trapped inside a black box. My mother tried not to panic and pressed on.

After about a half an hour of this, they felt a presence behind them. Unsure of what it was—it could have been anything from a bear to a wild boar to one of the many soldiers roaming the area, searching for escapees—they continued for a little further.

"Maya, we are going to die out here," my mother said once she'd realized that they were making no progress. "We will never make it through the night. Let's just sit here next to the road and wait for the morning to come so we can see where we are." She tried to warm my sister up from the cold and dampness of the night—as well as from pure terror, too. They had nothing with them except for the clothes on their backs, and the shorts and t-shirts they had on weren't exactly warm. They hadn't anticipated the nights in the mountains being as cold as they were, and my mother cursed herself for leaving her suitcase behind with that treacherous woman.

They sat along the side of the road waiting for dawn to shed light on a place to hide. As soon as the first light crept over the horizon, they started to walk again. They would throw themselves in a ditch whenever they heard army trucks approaching. My mother knew that the soldiers would be very suspicious of them if they were caught up on the mountain so near the border, so she came up with something to say in case they were spotted.

"Listen, Maya, if the soldiers catch us, we will tell them that some men driving a white car took us and that they wanted to rape us but were able to fight them off, and that they dumped us here and left us to die," my mother whispered, coaching my sister as best she could.

"Okay, Mami," my sister agreed.

"Maya, you *must* remember this story so that we don't look suspicious, okay?"

"Yes, Mami, I will," my sister replied, acknowledging the importance of their stories matching up if they were caught.

They continued to walk along the side of the winding road as the sun grew brighter and brighter, hiding every time they heard the sound of a car. They tried to be discreet when a jeep drove by, but this time the soldiers inside of it saw them and quickly made their way toward them.

"Hey, what's going on here?" one of them shouted at them. My mother kept her nerve and told them their invented story.

The soldiers fired question after question at them, but seemed to believe my mother's story. "Okay, ladies, which type of car was it? What color of car? How many people, and what did they look like?"

"We don't know the type of the car...the only thing I know is that it was white. They were two men, and we just started to fight with them and then they let us go." My mother didn't have to try to look shaken up by the fake ordeal; she was busy worrying about whether the soldiers would ask to see their expired papers.

The soldiers told them to get into the jeep and then they started to drive down the winding forest road to the bottom of the mountain.

"I will take you to the police station so you can give a statement of what happened to you," one of them informed my mother.

"No, please, we don't want to go to the police station!" she pleaded, knowing that if they did they would be exposed for sure.

"But I have to bring you there. Don't you want to make a statement?" the young man replied, confused.

Throughout the drive, my mother desperately tried to talk her way out of it by making small talk with the soldiers. They seemed receptive to her attempts at conversation, and one of the soldiers revealed that he was extremely happy to finish his shift because his wife just gave birth to a son and he couldn't wait to get home. My mother congratulated him on the birth, and they continued to talk about life and family and work.

"I work at a gas station in Slovakia where I make quite a bit of money. You should come and see us there some time and we will show you around," my mother said, trying to keep his mind off taking them to the police station while subtly letting him know that escaping wasn't on her mind.

"Do you want to see my passport? Here it is," she continued, casually shoving the sought-after document his way. She hoped that by offering to show the soldier her documents, he would assume that they were current—miraculously, it worked. He didn't want to see it at all, believing that she was telling him the truth.

"Listen, girls, what are you going to do at the police station?" the soldier said once they'd reached town. "They will not find the person anyway. You are probably very hungry. Let me take you home, feed you, and you can meet my little boy, yes?" My mother and sister nodded with enthusiasm, relieved that my mother's conversation had changed the soldiers' minds.

Luck had prevailed yet again.

As promised, the man took them to his humble abode where he explained their misfortune to his wife. She welcomed them with open arms and happily served them some fish, the couple's very cute baby balanced on her hip. Once their bellies were full, he took them to the bus station because my mother had told him that the reason they were hitchhiking in the first place was to meet a friend of hers at the motor rest.

"Girls, here is some money. Please don't hitchhike again! It is very dangerous," the soldier pleaded with them. "Take the bus."

Having emerged unscathed from this very narrow escape, my mother and sister stayed at the bus station until he was nowhere to be seen and then immediately made their way to the major highway where they hitchhiked back to the motor rest again without incident.

Testing Path to Paradise

The driver took them right back to where they had started from the previous day. They sat down in the coffee shop and ordered a coffee. After a few moments had passed, they noticed three men smiling at them from a few tables away.

"Hey girls," a waiter said as he passed their table, "those men are inviting you for coffee at their table if you are interested."

"No, Mami, we shouldn't!" my sister warned.

"Listen," my mother hissed back. "These people know the roads through the mountains that lead to Greece—they can help us!"

"No, Mami, we shouldn't," my sister tried again, worried, but my mother knew that those sorts of places were a source of knowledge for anyone wishing to escape, and that the men could possibly help them. It was a risk, but time was running out.

As she was arguing with my sister, a police car drove by the coffee shop. My mother glanced at the car and then back at my sister.

"Maya, if the police come in here and they ask us for our papers, we are done! Do you understand me?"

My sister relented. "Okay, Mami, let's go. Quickly!"

They stood up and walked toward the three men. They must have known that something was suspicious about my mother and sister, since they didn't seem to want to sit with them before the police car drove by but approached soon after it had passed.

"You ladies afraid of the police?" one of the men said in a teasing tone, but his eyes were serious.

"No, no...we just changed our minds," my mother said with a smile. One of the other men winked at her, as if to say that his companion wasn't to be trusted, so my mother and sister stayed silent until the man who had spoken abruptly got up, glanced at them one last time, and left.

"We don't trust that guy," the winking man said once their companion had gone.

"My name's Drago," said the other man at the table. "You want to escape, yes?"

"Yes, we do," my mother replied, wary but exhausted and out of options. She told the two men their story for what seemed like the thousandth time.

"I thought so," Drago said, leaning back in his chair. "I knew it was you because there was a woman who came here yesterday asking if anyone had seen two women who wanted to escape."

My mother and sister sat there in shocked disbelief silence, thinking back to the woman they had trusted with their things.

"Yes, it's true. She had short black hair with a tattoo of a cross on her right hand. She was asking where the police station was because there were two women who wanted to escape that had come to her for help. We told her where the police station was. You should be extra careful now," Drago added.

"Oh my God!" my mother said, taken aback by the woman's actions. Why would someone care so much about ratting out a mother just trying to find her daughter?

"Are you Catholic or Muslim?" Drago asked suddenly, changing the direction of the conversation.

"I am Catholic," she answered, puzzled.

Drago seemed to relax further into his chair. "I am Catholic as well, and that's why I will help you," he said. "A friend of mine escaped through here many years ago and now lives in Thessaloniki. He has all of his papers now. He is an architect. He will help you. His name is Christos. I will give the day off to my secretary, and you can stay in my office for the night."

They left the coffee shop right away and he drove them to the tiny factory he managed, pigs casually roaming around the yard. He called Christos and told him that he needed his help. Christos said that he would be there first thing in the morning.

"I will lock the door, and you can stay here," Drago said. With a parting smile, he closed the door, and my mother and sister were left alone.

My poor mother was petrified. She didn't know if the police would come and arrest them in the morning. She'd put all her trust in this man that she had met not even an hour ago. But there was no other choice. She had to trust somebody. There was absolutely no way of getting through the mountains as blindly as they had tried to do the night before.

They stayed in the tiny office all night, occasionally nibbling on the bread that Drago had left for them, petrified of what was to come. Needless to say, they didn't sleep much.

After what seemed like an endless night, the morning came with the sound of keys at the door. Trembling from fear, my mother and sister stood in a corner staring at the door, unsure of what was coming for them.

Luckily, they had trusted the right person. The door swung open, and Drago and another man entered.

"This is Christos," Drago said, gesturing to the other man. "He escaped many years ago, as I told you, and will show you the way through the mountains."

They left the office and drove to the motor stop to have breakfast, which my mother couldn't swallow from all the adrenalin rushing through her veins.

"Don't worry, everything will be fine," Drago said, trying to give her some courage. "We will all go now so that I can show you the way, and then you will leave in the evening. It's important not to go at midnight, which would attract too much attention from the army guys, but if you go around ten in the evening, you will be okay." All my mother and sister could do was nod, grateful and fearful at once.

Christos, Drago, my mother, and my sister made their way around the pit stop where the actual border was just a few scant meters away. The curved road continued on uphill and took them to a small forest next. They walked along the side of this dirt road for about a half an hour, and eventually they encountered a huge sign on the right-hand side reading, NO CROSSING: YOU WILL BE SHOT.

Christos turned to my mother. "Right after this sign, there will be some bushes through the forest there. You have to get through the bushes, and then you will end up in a vineyard. You will go through the grape vines and end up in a grassy field. Right after the field, you will see cars passing by on a road. That is Greece. I will be waiting for you on that road. I will flash my headlights to let you know that I am there waiting. You have to hide in the grape vines just before the field—kneel down there and wait for my headlights. Once you see my flashing headlights, you run for your life. Don't look behind you and run as quickly as you can and get in my car."

My mother and sister listened to all of this gravely, not wanting to miss a single detail. This was their shot. They couldn't miss it.

Christos continued on by telling my mother about the army base right next to the forest, with guard dogs that sniffed out unwanted guests. It was extremely important not to go in the dead of night, because in the early evening, chickens, rabbits, and squirrels were still scurrying and scratching around—the dogs barked at these noises all the time, and the guards were less likely to suspect escapees during this time because of this.

"Remember what I told you and follow my directions," Christos said once more on their way back, getting ready to part from them to drive across the border.

"Thank you!" my mother cried, clasping his hand. "Thank you so much. Christos, Drago, I will pray for you every day and thank God that he put you in our path."

They waited anxiously with Drago until evening arrived.

Ten o'clock. It was time.

Drago and my mother tried to appear like a young couple casually strolling around in order not to attract any undesirable attention, and my sister trailed behind. Once they were out of sight, they started to walk down the dirt road. The guard dogs began to bark just as Christos had said they would. It was very unnerving and it felt like they were right there beside their ankles, ready to bite. Christos had also instructed my mother on how to walk—very soft footsteps from the heel to the tiptoes, as quietly as possible.

"Drago, Drago, I am so afraid," my mother whispered as they picked their way through the forest. "Please, let's go back. I can't do this, they will shoot us!" She clenched his arm as tightly as she could, my sister doing the same.

He only gave her a stern look, shook their hands from his arm, and continued walking in silence, leaving my poor mother and sister trying to catch up as quietly as they could. There was no going back now. He had risked his life to help them—he could have been shot on the spot along with them if found. My mother and sister swallowed their fear and continued on.

They slowly and quietly made their way through the thick forest, bushes, and grape vines, still hearing the barking dogs behind them. Finally they ended up at the edge of the empty field.

They were now only 200 meters or so from the road that would lead them to freedom.

"Okay, sit here and wait for Christos to come," Drago said quietly. He turned to make his way back.

"Drago, thank you, thank you so much! I will pray that you get home safely...thank you," my mother whispered to him, adrenaline pumping in her veins.

Drago smiled. "Just be quiet and don't worry. I will be fine." With that, he left them.

They sat there in silence, waiting for their destiny to arrive.

It seemed like they spent an eternity watching the cars pass by. Suddenly, they saw the flashing lights in the distance. My mother grabbed my sister's hand and they both started to run as quickly as they could through the field without looking back. The headlights were getting closer and closer, and then they reached the car, opened the door, and tumbled in—trembling, breathless, ecstatic, and bawling.

"Thank you, thank you so much Christos!" they both cried.

"No, get down! Get down, we are not safe yet," Christos whispered urgently as he drove off. "They can still snap us up here. You have to put your heads down."

It was one o'clock in the morning when Christos stopped the car a few kilometers later and told them they could get out. Even through the darkness of the night, they were struck by the pure beauty of their surroundings as they got out of the car.

"Paradise...we are in paradise!" My mother said, weeping and jumping from joy alongside my sister.

The sweet smell of lavender and Calliandra flowers enveloped them as they gazed out at the quaint blue-and-white Greek houses before them.

That was it. They had made it, a journey five years in the making.

Overjoyed, they got back into the car and Christos drove them a bit further down the road. They stopped in a little store and he bought them a watermelon, which they devoured, and some unfamiliar Greek food for them to eat such as souvlaki, feta, spanakopita, and pita bread. They could finally enjoy a meal with peaceful hearts.

With the dangers of Yugoslavia behind them, my mother and sister entered a completely unknown world that spoke in what was to them a very strange language. It had been easy to communicate in Yugoslavia since Yugoslavians speak a Slavic language very close to Slovak. But here in the land of the gods, they were completely lost.

Christos drove for an additional hour and brought them to his office in Thessaloniki, which was around 50 kilometers from the border they had just crossed. There, he told them that ultimately they needed to make their own way to Athens, which was an additional 500 kilometers from Thessaloniki. It was only in Athens that political asylum was granted, and they were still in a little danger in Thessaloniki.

About an hour later, to my mother's total surprise, Drago arrived.

"Oh my God, Drago, I was so worried for your safety!" she cried, hugging him tightly. "If they had found you and killed you I would have never forgiven myself. I am so happy that you are alive. I cannot thank you enough. I will pray for you eternally."

"You are welcome, but I need you to know something," Drago said. "Once you arrive in Athens, the authorities will ask you to show them on the map where you came from. I am only asking of you that you do not tell them the truth. Don't even tell them you came from Gevgelia. If you do, you will make it much more difficult for others who want to escape. That is the only thing I want from you."

They agreed on this, and then spent a bit of time together until Christos and Drago let them rest for the remainder of the night.

At dawn, Drago and Christos drove them to the main road, which led to the highway. They gave them drachma, the official Greek money at the time, and instructed them to get in a car with only one driver and to tell the driver "Athens." After many hugs and tears, they bid them good luck and parted ways with my mother and sister.

Hence, with no skill in the local language whatso-ever, they made their way to a car that stopped for them shortly after Christos and Drago departed.

"*Pou*?" (Where?), the driver asked kindly.

"Athens, Athens," they replied.

"*Pou Athens*?" (Where in Athens?), the driver asked, trying to understand where exactly they wanted to go, since Athens is a huge city of millions of people.

"Athens...? Athens," they replied desperately. The confused driver, letting his attempts for more specific information go unanswered, drove off toward Athens with my mother and sister in tow.

At some point on the five-hour drive to Athens, my mother noticed something of importance to her as a believer in God. Some Greek people have a habit of christening themselves when they pass by a church—every church. Their driver was doing so every time they drove past a church on the side of the road.

"Maya, this man will not hurt us. He always christens himself when he sees a church," she told my sister in relief.

"*Na fame, na fame*?" (Eat, eat?), he asked them when they stopped at a pit stop with a restaurant. They shook their heads to let him know that they didn't understand what he was saying. He put his hand toward his mouth to show them what he meant and said, "*ham, ham*?" My mother understood this gesture, and they got out of the car and accompanied him into the restaurant, where he showed them the choices by pointing toward the desired food, and then they pointed in turn to what they wanted.

They continued on toward Athens after filling their bellies.

"*Pou Athens*?" the driver asked again as they entered the huge, illuminated city, as if they had somehow learned a new language in three hours. It was around ten o'clock in the evening.

"Athens," they said again, not knowing what else to say.

"*Pou Athens?*" the driver tried again in frustration.

"Athens, Athens," they repeated, and the man shook his head and drove on.

As if to officially welcome them to the capital, he dropped them off in front of the Athenian parliament building. It was a beautiful, rectangular-shaped building with stairs on each end. In the middle, two tiny booths a few meters apart sheltered guards, called Evzones, who stood motionless and silent at their posts. They were dressed in very peculiar clothing. They wore—and still do—white tights and a crimped kilt made of 30 meters of fabric with 400 pleats symbolizing the 400 years of living under Turkish rule. They also wore white shirts with long, wide, fluffy sleeves, an embroidered black-and-gold vest, a cute little circular red hat called a Fez, and stiff, pointy leather shoes with a large woolen ball on top of each one where a sharp blade would be hidden in the times when they were still a combat unit.

They stood in front of parliament, clueless as to what to do next.

"Where are we going to go?" my mother asked my sister, as if she somehow knew the answer. They saw police officers not too far from them just then, and my mother had a rather rash idea.

"Maya, let's break a window and they will put us in jail, and we can sleep there!"

"No, Mami, let's not do that," my sister answered, knowing that my mother was tired and not thinking straight.

They started approaching people who were passing by and saying, "*Politic asylum? Politic asylum*?" to anyone who would listen. Most people shook their heads and continued on. At last they had luck with a young blonde woman, who to their surprise ended up being Russian. Thank God! They could communicate at last with someone who could understand them, since Russian is closer to Slovak than Greek will ever be. Both of them did speak a little Russian, as well, since they came from a Communist country where Russian was mandatory in schools.

"Okay, I will take you to the police station, and they will help you there," said the blonde woman with sympathy.

Once they arrived at the police station, the officers asked them for their visas, which obviously they didn't have, as my mother kept repeating "*politic asylum*" to the bewildered officers. I think that the officers decided to try to lighten the mood a bit by attempting to joke with my sister, and perhaps flirt a little. Maya was quite a stunning young girl then, and she grew to become a gorgeous woman inside and out later on. One of the police officers put his hand on her shoulder as if to console her, and said, "don't worry, Gustav Husak, Gustav Husak," perhaps as an attempt at a joke. At the time, the Slovak president was Gustav Husak.

"No Gustav Husak, no Gustav Husak!" my sister yelled, confusing him. The language barrier was clearly too much to overcome.

My sister then tried her luck with talking to them in Italian, which she'd learned a little of in Split when she got together with that young Italian guy. Right away they called the Italian embassy to get a translator for them. Once the translator arrived my sister somehow succeeded to explain that they had escaped through the mountains and that they want to go to Canada. At that point the officers understood exactly what was going on, and put a map in front of them to ask them from where they'd come—a situation that Drago had warned them about. Remembering this, they pointed on the map to a completely different area, and that was the end of it.

The officers, realizing that the two must be hungry, combined their money and went to buy some yogurt, souvlaki, and salads for my mother and sister to eat. Before leaving, they had them sit in a jail cell, communicating in hand gestures that they were not under arrest but that they could sleep there for the night.

In the morning they were woken up by one of the officers, who gestured at them to follow him. He brought them to the immigration office, which was packed with numerous Polish defectors waiting for their papers to travel to Australia, the United States, or Canada.

"Maya, thank God we ended up here," my mother said to my sister, relieved. "At least we can talk to someone who will understand us." Polish is closer to Slovak than to Greek, and my mother figured that she could get along if she had to.

"How did you learn such a complicated language as Greek?" my mother asked one of the Polish men who was hanging around the premises.

"Don't worry, you will learn very quickly," he replied with a smile. "It's quite easy once you start."

The immigration office provided them—as they did for other political refugees—one week's stay in a hotel. The office had provided us with six months of accommodations when my father and I had come through Greece, but then again I was a young child, and my sister was in her late teens and therefore capable of taking care of herself more adequately. Perhaps the laws had changed during the five years in between our escape and my mother and sister's escape.

Ironically, my mother and sister stayed in the same hotel where I had stayed just five years earlier—hotel Arcadia. My father was very smart to take me with him when he fled for the simple reason that I was his golden ticket to opening doors everywhere, since people were less likely to leave a young child on the streets.

The immigration office gave them some money for food to last them a week or so, and then they were on their own, sleeping on the street or the park if they needed to after their one-week stay in the hotel.

"Ask people for Omonia, a very famous marketplace for shopping. It's a huge square where all the immigrants come together—people will show you where it is. Perhaps someone will help you find a job. Remember, you only have a week," one of the workers informed them just before they left.

They immediately walked to Omonia in the hopes of finding some much-needed work, since they only had a week to do so.

A few years earlier, my mother's cousin Kornel had managed to escape from Slovakia and was staying in Greece somewhere, but my mother was clueless as to where exactly he might be. She asked the same lady who'd informed her about Omonia whether she knew of someone by that name, but the lady kindly told her that she couldn't divulge any information about anyone since it was confidential.

Imagine the coincidence that, in a city of eight million people, my mother sat down at a table in a little café in Omonia next to four Polish men who ended up knowing her cousin Kornel.

Initiating the first move, my mother started conversing with them. They told her how they had escaped on a ship in the middle of the night. They had sneaked up on the ship, hid in the bottom where the engines were, and waited for a couple of days until it was safe to go out. The captain of the ship nearly had a heart attack when he saw them emerging from below deck, dirty and black as charcoal and asking him to let them off on one of the Greek islands. Now the men were waiting in Greece to get to the United States.

My mother asked them if they knew of any potential jobs that she could do without speaking the language.

"Okay, yes, I know someone who needs somebody to iron their clothes," one of them said to her. His name was Tomek, and he was the head of the four young men's group. He used to be a bodyguard, and my mother said that he was quite a witty, smart guy.

Now, that year in Greece there was a huge heat wave during which many died from the agonizing temperatures trapped within the city's cement buildings. So she went to work for this man in the basement of a house in 43° C heat with no air conditioning. To this day she has trouble with her feet burning due to the remnants of that extremely hot time ironing clothes in Athens.

After a while ironing clothes, she couldn't endure the heat any longer—she was sure that she would die of heat stroke. She decided to buy herself a dictionary, and since there was no Slovak-to-Greek dictionary, she bought a Polish-to-Greek one. Little by little, in that terrible heat while ironing t-shirts for peanuts, she translated the Polish words to Slovak and then to Greek, sometimes asking the boys for help for the words she couldn't understand from the dictionary. The boys happily explained the incomprehensible words to my mother, who never lost her drive to learn. She started to create her own dictionary and asked the boys to translate simple sentences like "My name is...", "Where is this?", "I

want...", "I don't want....", "I am going home...", "Where
is the Metro?" and so on.

Every day, she stepped up to her challenges and
quickly learned more and more of the important phrases
she needed to know in order for her to be able to survive
as well as thrive in her new life.

"Celia, you are going to leave me very soon, yes?" the
old man she worked for kept asking her kindheartedly
when he saw how swiftly she was learning Greek.

Their time at the hotel came to an end quickly, and
my mother went to Tomek for his help. He offered them
a mattress in his own place, as he'd come to care deeply
for my mother. He had told her on many occasions that if
he had to have her as a wife, he definitely would have died
from laughter since my mother's language was so funny
to him.

The place where he stayed was a sort of dorm—a long
hallway with many rooms and at the end of it a small
kitchen that they all shared. Tomek and the boys kindly
let them sleep on a mattress on the floor in one of the
rooms. Accommodations thus secured for the time being, my mother continued on her path of learning.

One day she asked Tomek about her cousin, thinking
that it was next to impossible that he knew of him but that
it was worth asking about, anyway.

"Tomek, listen, I have a cousin here in Greece who
escaped from Slovakia a couple of years ago. The immigration office didn't want to give me his address, but I
know that he is here somewhere."

"Yes, we saw one Slovak guy around here…I wonder if he's the man you're looking for? He is always drunk and doesn't work," Tomek answered, clearly not impressed with this man he'd seen.

My mother was both heartened and frustrated by this news. "Yes, it's probably him," she sighed, knowing very well that Nadia, Kornel's sister, was sending him money, which he was clearly wasting on the bottle.

"You should go to the café where we were—he's around there quite often drinking beer."

My mother and my sister kept going to that café until one day she noticed a skinny man with a familiar face. In a city of millions, there was Kornel.

"Kornel!" she yelled to him.

"Celia!" he yelled back when he saw her, surprised. They approached each other and began to get reacquainted after so many years apart.

"Where do you live now that you're in Athens?" she asked him.

"I'm…renting a balcony," he informed her. It seemed that he had drank away all of his money as she'd suspected. That year it was hot enough for a person to live outside without a problem, at least. They continued to catch up for a while, but there was not much to say since it was clear that he was wasting his life away with booze. They said that they would be sure to see each other soon and then parted ways.

"Celia, I will find you work at the school if you want me to, as a cleaning lady," Tomek said to my mother one day when he saw how rapidly she was learning Greek. "And since students have their food paid for, you can distribute sandwiches to them, as well." He was a driver for the American school in Kifisia, 15 kilometers from Athens. My mother heartily agreed to his plan.

Once she arrived and rolled up her sleeves to work on her first day, she realized that the place was completely spotless—even the floors were shining like stars in the sky, and my mother was curious as to what exactly she was supposed to be doing there. It seemed that her work had already been done for her. She swept, but there was nothing to sweep. She nevertheless was extremely appreciative to have this job, especially because the school had air conditioning.

"Celia, do you want to go work in a bar?" Tomek asked her a couple of days later, seeing that she was bored out of her mind at the school—there must have been little elves who came at night and cleaned up the place for her.

"What the heck am I going to do in a bar when I don't know anything about bartending?" she asked him.

"What? Are you kidding? It's easy," Tomek laughed. "You will sit there behind the bar and they will ask you for mostly *Katistar*. *Katistar* is easy: you put ice, then the alcohol, and voilà! And on top of it, they will give you tips."

"And that's it?" my mother asked.

"Yeah, that's it," he concluded, seemingly very proud of himself for having had this idea.

So she went to work in a bar until two o'clock in the morning most nights and continued to work at the American school during the day, where she ended up in the broom closet catching up on sleep more often than not. There were three other girls already working at the bar. The trick was to converse with the male customers until they offered to buy you a drink, and then the bar manager gave the girls water instead of alcohol.

Life during this time seemed like paradise. They went to the immigration office monthly to check on their status, where they met a few people who were ready to leave to their new homes. These same people would write them periodically, letting them know about their new lives wherever they ended up as well as letting them know not to push so hard to get out. Their pen pals urged them to enjoy their life in Golden Greece and their status as immigrants while they still could because once they left, life in their new countries was a little bit harsher. Trying to make a new life for yourself was a huge challenge, and people got used to a type of lifestyle in Greece only to be hit with a reality check when they reached places like the United States or Canada.

So my mother enjoyed her time in Greece as much as she could. She worked at night at the bar making good money, and continued to work at the American school during the day, which ended at four o'clock. My sister and mother went out together, ate watermelons and souvlaki, and went to little coffee shops and gorgeous Mediterranean beaches. Life was sweet and exciting.

Never would they have left magnificent Greece if it hadn't been for me.

— —

One day, my mother wrote to Caesar that she wanted him to send me to Greece. He of course refused, and told me nothing about my mother's whereabouts or even her existence.

"But what I can do is sponsor you, so that you will only have to wait for one year instead of two," my father told my mother over the phone, "and then we can get re-married once you get here, put the family back together." This, of course, wasn't his intention at all, as my father had met a woman during this time and things had begun to get serious with her.

My mother agreed, swallowing her disgust in order to see me again. And so they bided their time, living and working in Greece while the year passed by.

In the meantime, my mother met a young Greek woman while working at the American school by the name of Sofia, who was the daughter of a very famous singer in Greece. Sofia and her brother shared a beautiful apartment together in a nice part of the city.

Wanting to help my sister with meeting new friends, my mother decided to introduce her to Sofia, and they hit it off right away. Shortly after, Sofia asked my sister if she was interested in living with her and her brother, and Maya decided to take them up on it.

Maya had already found a new and exciting path for herself in that jungle of a city, as well. She was working in a classy bar in Glyfada making beautiful cocktails in the evening and modeling during the day.

The modeling job she got partly thanks to a man they had met when they had just arrived in Athens and were sipping on refreshments at a café. He was a young man named Ludek, Czech by nationality, who informed Maya that he'd seen an ad in the newspaper looking for models and that he thought Maya should apply, as God had surely made her to be a model. She had everything working for her: tall, skinny, long blondish hair, and hazel eyes. She was and is just plain gorgeous.

So she went to the agency—still wearing her torn-up t-shirt from their escape—to make an official portfolio, and they wanted her to work for them right away. She would look good in a potato sack, my sister.

One evening, while working at the bar, my mother met a man by the name of Manolis. After a few weeks of courting, he asked her to come and live with him and not waste money at the dorm, which she gladly agreed to.

Life was great in the land of the gods. My sister and mother were thriving in their new lives.

One day, Tomek came to see my mother at the bar. He was spitting mad.

"Listen, Celia," he said, "we gave your cousin a place to stay, and all he needed to do was cook for us, and then he goes and steals our money! We saved for a year to get this money together to take with us to the United States, and he takes it! We had $100,000! Tell him to give it back!"

"No, it cannot be true, did he really...?" my mother said in pure disbelief.

"Yes, it is. I know it was him, and if he doesn't give it back we will find him. We will beat him up and call his sister to get the money. And if she doesn't give it to us, we will kill him, cut him into tiny pieces, and send him to his sister like that," Tomek said, shocking my mother with his vicious words.

My poor mother went looking for Kornel in the streets of Athens. She found him in one of the coffee shops that Tomek didn't frequent as much.

"Kornel," she said, "you have to give that money back! What were you thinking? What have you done? They will kill you if you don't give it back!"

"I didn't steal any money!" he told her, clearly lying.

"Yes, you did. I know it was you, and *they* know it was you. You have to give it back! They also know that you are going to Vancouver. They will find you there in Canada and they will kill you. Those guys worked hard for a year to gather that money and you go and steal it? How could you?"

"Celia...I don't have it anymore," he sighed, his expression one of desperation.

"What do you mean you don't have it? Give me their money and I will give it back to them," she told him, sickened and embarrassed by what he had done.

"Celia, you will not believe me when I tell you. I was drunk, and I put the money in my back pocket. Then a little gypsy girl passed behind me, went in my pocket, and took it! I couldn't run after her...I was too drunk," he said, shame in his voice and on his face.

"Kornel, you are done. They will kill you for sure," she said. He just sat there in silence. "Okay, I will help you," she reluctantly said to him after a couple of minutes. He was, after all, family, even though she struggled with whom to give her devotion and support to as Tomek had helped her immensely from the beginning. But Kornel was family, and he needed her help, so she hid him in the apartment she shared with her boyfriend until he had his visa for Vancouver.

Manolis drove him to the airport on his departure day, and Kornel arrived in Vancouver where his sister was awaiting for him. Unfortunately, his days were numbered, because the police found him dead one day not too long after his arrival. Foul play, they said. My mother was sure that the polish boys had found out where he lived and killed him for what he had done.

⟶ ⟶

After a year of living and waiting, the papers arrived, and it was time to leave their lives in Greece behind and embark on a new journey to Canada.

With Western jitters and Greek blues, they sat on the airplane together. A little over a year had passed since their escape, and more than seven since my father took me. I was now sixteen years old.

Familiar Entity

September 1988

While my mother was on her way to Canada from her life in Greece, my father lied to me and told me that my mother was in jail. I had no clue of how she'd ended up there in the first place, and he wouldn't tell me anything more when I pressed him about it. This was all I knew.

"Do you want to go and see Bernsie in Montreal?" he asked me one Friday evening, just a couple of days after informing me about my mother's predicament. He sounded uncharacteristically nervous.

Bernsie had been my good friend since shortly after my arrival in Montreal, and I missed her once we moved two hours away to Shawinigan. We were both nine when we met, and she wasn't a good friend at first. She and her brother would make me repeat silly things in French—I spoke none of it and it must have been funny for them to hear me mumble whatever they wanted me to repeat.

A few years later, we'd grown up a bit and she became my best friend. We used to get into trouble together. One time we took revenge on one of my father's girlfriends, whom I hated since she wanted nothing to do with me at all.

Bernsie and I "borrowed" the girlfriend's car and took it for a joy ride; unfortunately for us, the neighbors told on us and we got in quite a lot of trouble. But the revenge was sweet nonetheless, and we laughed about it for years to come. She was my partner in crime in all aspects of my life. She was my confidant and the best friend a girl could ever have. We spent every day together, and I would sleep over at her house as often as I could.

We even shared boyfriends—or rather shared their time, alternating hanging out with them week to week. When we were twelve, she declared that her boyfriend at the time should kiss me because my experience in that field was still nonexistent. She said that he was a good kisser, and that she wanted my first kiss to be a good one. The kiss itself was more of peck than the sweepingly romantic kiss we all yearn for when we're that age, but it was still a nice gesture.

Needless to say, my father knew very well that I would be ecstatic to go and see Bernsie when he offered.

"Oh yes, I can't wait!" I said, excited at the prospect. I went to bed, and that night I heard my father up pacing around, but I didn't think anything of it at the time.

The next day we were off on the road to Montreal. My father smoked like a chimney during the whole two-hour trip. He was really quiet; much too quiet to my liking. I knew a storm was brewing when he was deep in thought like that, and it looked like this one was going to be a hurricane.

We parked the car in front of Bernsie's house and I ran to the door, rang the buzzer. The door clicked open and I climbed the few stairs of the duplex, the upstairs door swinging open as I ascended.

When I looked up, I saw something inconceivable.

It was my mother.

The woman I'd been praying for for all those years, the woman whom I thought had abandoned me, a ghost from the past, a vision—was standing right in front of me. With tears running down her face and her arms wide open to me, she cried "Celinka!" Just one word, that beautiful word—the sweetest sound from a mother's mouth is your name. I had not heard her voice in seven years, and now she was standing right in front of me, saying it. I couldn't believe it—*this must be a hallucination*, I thought to myself.

I found out later on that Caesar had told my mother he would wait for them at the airport, which he obviously didn't follow through on. My poor mother arrived with a lot of mixed emotions about coming to Canada—sorrow for leaving her charmed life in Greece behind and pure euphoria for the idea of seeing her daughter at last after seven years apart. She arrived in Montreal expecting to see me there at the airport and instead she was faced with the possibility that my father had yet again betrayed her.

Instead of going himself, Caesar had sent his best friend, Pavel—who was also Bernsie's father—to take my mother and sister to Pavel and Bernsie's house. He was a very strange phenomenon, this Pavel. He was quite tall, very bulky, with curly brown hair down his neck, a thick beard, and a raspy, deep voice from too many cigarettes. He looked like a younger version of Santa Claus. My father told Pavel what my mother and sister looked like and where to pick them up, which he thankfully did. When Pavel picked them up he informed them that Caesar was busy and couldn't make it—one more jab at my mother's already frayed nerves.

Bastard!

When I saw her standing in the doorway to Bernsie's duplex, I threw myself into her arms. Right at that moment, my father took a picture of us, which I still have hanging on my wall in my house. We embraced, cried, and held each other tightly for a long time, trying to make up for the years we'd been apart all at once. She had come back to me. She had found a way. She wasn't in jail or dead, and she hadn't abandoned me. She was real, and I knew that my life would be filled with love again now that she was here. Happiness and confusion overwhelmed me in equal parts, and I remember thinking that this had to be the happiest day of my life.

For all the trouble that would follow, at least I had my mother with me again in that moment.

After the initial jubilation, I saw that my sister was in the living room, too. She got up from the sofa bed in the living room where they were sleeping and we hugged politely. We didn't quite know what to say to each other;

too much time had passed, and it was awkward between us. She was so beautiful—unlike me, the ugly duckling still to become a swan.

As we began to talk, I realized that my mother didn't speak a word of English, and since my father had told me to forget everything that had to do with Slovakia, I'd forgotten most of my native tongue, as well. Needless to say, communication between us was extremely difficult. We tried to speak to each other, but our new lack of a common tongue made it a very frustrating task. After a while we just contemplated each other, inspecting every corner of each other's faces and trying to take back what had been taken from us.

We stayed at Bernsie's for a few more hours, and then we set off on the trip back to Shawinigan. I could see that my father was quite unhappy about this whole situation, and he must have known what was about to happen.

My mother stayed with us for a couple of days, and we continued to try to make up for lost time, but it was painful and confusing for me to be with both of them in the same space again with all of the flashbacks to our violent history to deal with.

Because of this, less than a week later I announced to my father that I was leaving with my mother and sister. We packed our bags, and he dropped us off at the bus station where we set off to Montreal. My father had given my mother the telephone number of a friend of his with whom we could stay until we found an apartment of our own. Everything seemed to be going well so far. I suppose

I should have been more suspicious of my father letting us go so easily.

The very next day, my mother and sister found themselves a job in a Greek restaurant as they both spoke Greek (but still no English). This endeared them to the owners of the restaurant, who welcomed them with open arms.

But their new life in this Promised Land was not what they had expected it to be. It was now October, and the smell of the harsh Canadian winter around the corner that you could feel in your bones made them yearn for their sweet life in Greece, where flowers still bloomed and the Mediterranean heat puts a smile on your face regardless of your situation. With the two of them depressed and missing the land of the gods and me only caring about staying with my mother, we all decided to go back to their paradise.

One evening, I came back to our small apartment next to the Greek restaurant to a much-too-familiar scene. My mother was sitting down on the couch, crying and shaking like a leaf in hurricane season. I could see the fear in her eyes, and I didn't understand what had happened to make her be in this state of mind, but the voice at the back of my mind—a voice that sounded a lot like my father's— quickly gave me a pretty good idea of the situation.

I sat down next to her, and she tried to explain what had happened with the few words that she and I both had in common.

"You bitch, you whore!" my father had screamed at her over the phone, angry with her because, in his eyes, she had stolen me away from him. I imagine that the irony of this was lost on him. My mother said that he promised to break her arms and her legs when he saw her next. She was utterly petrified by his outburst. It must have been a terrible reminder of her time with him back in Slovakia. It took me a while to console her, especially considering we still didn't speak the same language.

So we did what needed to be done: we packed our bags very quickly, left the apartment, and set off to the airport to go back to Greece. She still had her friend Manolis, and she said that he would let us stay with him and from there we could make a brand-new life together. Of course, I was ecstatic about this—I loved Greece, and was excited at the prospect of going back.

It would be a new beginning for us. First my mother and I would go, and then my sister would follow. We left Maya behind—who was eighteen years old at the time— until we amassed enough money to buy her a ticket to join us. In the meantime she would stay with the kind Greek restaurant owners' daughter, whom she had befriended. My sister was very eager to go back to Greece, as well, as she had a boyfriend she'd left behind and her modeling job to go back to.

And so, our hearts filled with hope, my mother and I landed in Greece. Upon arrival, the officials looked at her documentation, saw her Canadian visa, and asked her to follow them right away. While I was outside waiting, they put her in a room and asked her why she had a

Canadian visa and was back in Greece after only a month, knowing the answer all the time, of course.

Our lack of buying a return ticket gave away our intentions of staying in the country—a life-changing, bittersweet mistake. Or was it just our destiny calling to us? Since I believe that everything has a place in this universe, I will go with destiny.

The Greeks were extremely accommodating and lenient toward immigrants during this time, but once you left the country they expected you to stay at your destination and not come back until you had a valid passport and wanted to come back for a short vacation, for example. My mother, having grown used to the accommodating, helpful, funny, and kind people she'd met while living in Greece, was caught off guard by the unfriendly, harsh airport security personnel.

She tried to save herself with lies, but to no avail. They wanted to know why she was returning to Greece with Canadian landed immigrant status stamped in her Slovak passport. She told them that she had friends of hers who were waiting for her who had money for her as well—she didn't have enough money on her for their liking, and they were wondering how she planned to pay for her expenses while being in the country.

No matter what explanations my mother tried, they knew very well what she was up to since she wasn't the first or the last to try their hand at coming back to Golden Greece. Many immigrants quickly decided to come back to Greece in the hopes of returning to the sweet life they'd left behind once they'd lived for a little while in the States or Canada, only to be returned to their destination country, or worse, back to their country of origin. The immigration officers wanted to deport my mother back to Slovakia. At best she would have gone straight to jail for four years for defecting, but who knows what they would have done to her with the KGB looking for her.

Relentless and sassy, she continued to argue with the officials as hard as she could, telling them that since she had a Canadian visa and they wanted to deport her, they should at least extradite her back to Canada and not Slovakia. They agreed, and told her that it was up to her to pay for her own return ticket.

With our shattered dreams trailing behind us, we made our way to a phone and she called her friend Manolis to come and pick me up. For me, at least, it was no problem entering Greece since I had a valid Canadian passport. My mother, however, had no choice but to go back to Canada.

She handed me all the jewelry that she had on her, which consisted of a ring with Arabian pearls and diamonds as well as a beautiful bracelet to match. A customer from the bar in Greece where she'd worked not too long ago had given them to her. She also gave me a few of her other rings. Manolis was not very rich and he had absolutely no way of helping her financially for her ticket, so it was up to her to figure out a way to pay for her fare.

She instructed me to bring the jewelry to a friend of hers, Costa, in exchange for money, and she told me to convey her promise to pay it back plus interest once she got back to Canada if he would just hold the jewels for her. Unfortunately, she never saw her jewelry again as Costa secretly sold all of it in order to keep his business alive, which he eventually lost anyway.

"Celinka, you will stay with Manolis until I figure out what to do next and send you back to me. Don't worry, everything will be fine," she said to me, sounding surprisingly calm. She spoke in a mixture of English and Slovak, which she had started to teach me again.

She was a strong woman who had gone through thick and thin in order to get back to me, and this was nothing but a little speed bump on our road to healing our relationship. It was still very difficult to leave her.

There I was with a perfect stranger, about to embark on the next chapter of my life.

We came back the next day with the money—not as much as she had hoped for, but then again, this was her ticket to freedom. We hugged one last time while she told me that everything would be fine yet again. I tried to be strong for her. After our goodbyes were said, Manolis and I departed, leaving my poor mother to fend for herself within the prison walls of the airport.

I was in the land of the gods again, but not feeling like a goddess, I must admit. Manolis and I drove to his extremely noisy apartment in the middle of Athens, his tiny car barely running and huffing and puffing from every hole. I liked Manolis—he was a kind man, short, quite plump, and he had a son that he had custody of every so often. Regardless of enjoying the company of my new de facto guardian, I was still baffled by this whole situation.

Here I was, motherless again. So much had happened in such a short period of time. My mother came back into my life in a peculiar, inexplicable way only to be torn from me once again. I'd been set adrift by the winds of fate in a strange but at least somewhat familiar country, not knowing if or when I would see my mother or sister again and trusting a strange but thankfully kind man to care for me. Everything was unknown again, and the unknown was overwhelming. That night, in pure and utter hopelessness, I cried myself to sleep.

A New Chapter

While she waited on her fate, my mother was kept at the airport in a very secure area so she couldn't escape. Desperate and weeping, she stayed underneath the stairs all night. As she huddled there, she noticed an African woman with a cute little four-year-old child not too far from her. The African lady came over to see what was distressing my mother so much.

"Why are you crying?" the lady asked with a kind smile. "You should be happy. You are going to Canada. They are deporting me back to Somalia." Her face fell when she said the bit about Somalia, and my mother understood that she was trying to make her feel better by showing her that her situation could be much worse.

My mother, realizing that her predicament really wasn't as dire as it could be, decided to take her last piece of jewelry from around her neck and gently place it around the Somali woman's neck as a gesture of empathy.

"Thank you. Thank you so much," the Somali woman said to her, touching the necklace.

They stayed together for the rest of the night.

Nearly a week later, two police officers finally arrived and asked my mother to follow them. They were her escort to the plane that would take her back to Canada.

My mother is a resilient woman; she truly is the living embodiment of "if life gives you lemons, make lemonade." I was extremely proud of her during this time for being so brave, and I still am today.

But her journey was not finished yet; nor was mine. More battles had to be won.

The two officers escorted her to an Olympic Airways jet out on the tarmac. As she climbed the stairs of the structure leading up to the plane's open door, my mother could see the passengers' faces staring out at her through the windows of the plane, no doubt wondering who this woman being escorted by not one but two police officers was.

One of the officers handed my mother's passport to the head steward, a short, chubby man who was welcoming the passengers onto the plane. The officer instructed him to bring my mother and her passport to the immigration office once they had landed in Montreal.

Under the whispers and curious stares of the other passengers, she sat down and began to sob anew. The plane took off, leaving behind what seemed like her last hope of being together and happy with her children in a land she had grown to love.

The itinerary of the flight was Athens to Montreal, and then from Montreal to the final destination of Toronto.

While they flew, my mother was incapable of putting a single fork of food in her mouth from nerves, so she kept smoking one cigarette after another instead since you could still smoke on planes at the time. She didn't know how the Canadian officials would react to her for not wanting to stay in their country after she'd gone through so much to get there in the first place. *Why would they welcome back someone who clearly doesn't want to be there?* She thought to herself.

What was she going to do? They couldn't deport her back to Slovakia, could they? Where could she go? She couldn't go back to Montreal, since she'd deserted the apartment and my sister was already staying with the kind Greek family from the restaurant. She had to make a new plan. She needed to make her way to Toronto, where her first brother escaped about a year after we had, no one knowing how he'd done it. He was the black sheep of the family and was known to have a brute for a wife. Then again, my mother had no choice at this point, so she had to find a way to reach Toronto in the hopes of her brother welcoming her and helping her to get situated.

She sat there, chain-smoking and crying, until a curious Greek lady next to her decided to break the silence and sobs with a question.

"I'm sorry to disturb you, but I want to ask you something. What did you do that was so bad that you had two police officers escorting you to the plane?" the lady asked inquisitively.

"Nothing," my mother replied, wiping her nose with the back of the hand that held her cigarette. "I didn't like it so much in Canada and wanted to go back to Greece with my daughters. You see, my ex-husband kidnapped my younger daughter seven years ago, and I managed to escape to Greece with my older one. I liked it there but had to go to Canada to get my younger girl back from him, but we didn't want to stay in Canada, so I decided to come back to Greece with my girls, and they didn't let me in." Unable to hold them back, fresh sobs spilled out after she had finished telling this woman her story.

"And that's it?" the Greek passenger asked, perplexed.

"Yes, that's it," my mother answered. The poor lady was shaking her head, unable to understand why they would go to such lengths for a person who just wanted to live her life in Greece and to have her children close by.

A few minutes later, when my mother went to the bathroom, the steward asked her the same question. She told him the same story, and he too couldn't understand the radical measures of the two police escorts for such a minor situation.

"Listen," my mother said, fixing the steward with her emerald-green gaze, "couldn't you ask the pilot if instead of dropping me off in Montreal, he could take me on to Toronto? I have a brother there. I have no one in Montreal, and no money."

"Okay, I will ask him, but I can't guarantee that he'll say yes," he replied.

He came back not too long after this exchange and let her know that the pilot had agreed, and that there was enough space for her to stay for the trip to Toronto. My mother heaved a sigh of relief—one less headache. But she still needed to get her passport back since the stewards still had it and had been instructed to give it to an immigration officer in Montreal. Montreal was where passengers from their flight went through passport control as well as immigration, as theirs was an international flight. She knew that she probably couldn't go on to Toronto if she got off the plane in Montreal and went through customs.

They arrived in Montreal, where most people disembarked. The head steward told the nice steward who was trying to help her that my mother was supposed to get off here. The nice steward shook his head, telling him no, that she was continuing on with them to Toronto and that the pilot had agreed to this. My mother stayed seated, worried that the head steward would alert the immigration officials and that they would come and escort her off the plane at any moment. But luck was on her side that day; no one came to take her.

Her head pounding from the effort of so much thinking on her feet, she pressed her luck yet again once they were back up in the air.

"Hey, listen," she said to the steward, "I am begging you...do you think that you can help me one more time and persuade your boss to give me back my passport before we disembark? What if they decide to deport me back to Slovakia after all? I will die! I need my passport. Can you please help me?"

"Okay, wait a second, I will go talk to him," the easy-going man replied. She was grateful for his willingness to help.

He came back with the head steward a couple of minutes later.

"So," the head steward said to my mother, "what exactly did you do?"

Swallowing her fears, she recounted a summary of the whole story to him as he listened with interest.

"You know what? I hate police officers!" he hissed when she'd finished, shooting my mother a sly smile while eyeing the other steward as if to get some type of nonverbal approval from him. The other steward nodded.

"I will give it to her," the head steward said. "What did she do that was so bad? Nothing! She didn't like it here and wanted to go back to Greece. So what? We will give her back her passport!" he declared. My mother was astonished and delighted, and thanked the two stewards profusely.

Thank you, God! She said to herself as she got off the plane in Toronto, passport in hand. *Thank...you...God!*

Unwelcoming Committee Awaits

They landed at the busy Toronto airport. My mother disembarked, thanked them repeatedly, and slowly walked through the halls, still anxious about the possibility of getting caught. But since she was coming from Montreal and didn't need to go through customs, no one questioned her as she walked amidst the other travelers. She reentered Canada free as a bird.

"Where are you?" her brother asked, puzzled, once she'd called him from a phone booth at the airport.

"In Toronto," she answered wearily, for she knew that he wasn't the friendly type.

"Toronto? Where in Toronto?"

"At the airport," she answered, hesitant to tell him more just yet.

"Which airport? Which terminal? Ask someone and then tell me," he instructed. She grabbed a person who was passing by her and asked for help in her broken

English, handing him the phone so that he could explain where she was to her brother.

"Okay, I know where you are. Wait for me outside and don't go anywhere. I am coming soon," her brother said when the man had handed the phone back to her, and then he hung up.

Once he arrived and she had gotten in the car, he immediately started to lecture her.

"What have you gotten yourself into this time? You're making problems for everyone. Why are you inventing yourself problems, hmm? What? Did you have such a bad life in Montreal that you had to go back to Greece? And how the hell did you end up here?"

"Well, they deported me from Greece and I managed to get here," she explained nervously to her brother, who was throwing disapproving glances in her direction whenever his eyes weren't on the road.

"I would throw all of you out if I were them," he spat. "Instead of appreciating where you are, what are you doing? You want to go somewhere else." He continued his ranting all of the way to the apartment.

In a way, he had a point. People all over the world risk their lives to come to places where they can have a chance at a better life, and here was my mother wanting to go back to Greece just because Canada didn't agree with her. He didn't understand what exactly she was missing in Canada. But for my mother, who had gone through so much, she just wanted to get back to where she had made a new life for herself already—to where she felt safe, where the weather was pleasing, where she knew people. Starting over yet again in Canada seemed like just too much to get used to, and the pull of Greece was too strong.

They arrived at his apartment and were greeted by Olga, his wife. Without any hugs or smiles to greet her, my poor mother settled in with her head down and hands between her knees on the couch, listening to the constant badgering.

Everyone has family history. I won't go into detail on the "bad blood" between Olga, my uncle, and my mother, but suffice to say that Olga hated my mother and made sure to let her know it when she arrived at their apartment. Olga was a very negative, person. When my grandmother visited them in Canada a few years after they'd moved from Toronto, they both treated her like a slave and made her feel extremely unwelcome in their home. Olga even called my grandmother a whore to her face. She ended up calling my mother in a state of pure panic and despair, and my mother had to fly across the country to bring her back to Toronto. They never spoke again until my grandmother's death decades later.

While my mother was staying in her brother's apartment after her tearful return from Greece, my sister decided that she wanted to come and say goodbye to her before embarking on her own adventure back to Athens. My sister had already purchased her ticket and was leaving within a week. Learning from our mistake, she had purchased a return ticket so as not to attract any suspicions from the Greek authorities, and also had a substantial amount of money with her to help her start again in Greece.

My mother was delighted at the prospect of seeing her oldest daughter again before Maya left the country, and immediately said yes to Maya's idea of coming for a visit.

"Who was that on the phone?" Olga barked once my mother had hung up.

"It was Maya asking if she could come to say good-bye to me before going back to Greece. I told her that of course she could come," my mother answered.

"Absolutely not! How dare you tell her that she can come to my apartment?" Olga snapped, livid. "I don't want that spoiled, rude stray in my house!"

"Olga, it never crossed my mind that you would say no," my mother said, trying to diffuse Olga's rage. "Our kids used to play together in Slovakia. We spent many Sunday dinners together at my mother's house, remember? We are family."

"You don't get to decide whether she comes to visit here or not! How *dare* you make that decision? Is this your home? No! You're not in Slovakia anymore, missy. Here it is different. People don't just barge into peoples' houses *here*. What in the hell were you *thinking*?" Olga continued on like this for some time, completely wrapped up in her self-righteous rampage. My mother quickly gave up trying to interject, and decided to put her tail between her legs and stay calm instead.

After Olga's rant had finished, my mother went out into the hallway to be alone for a while. There, she met a very kind Czech woman named Ivy, who was a resident in the same complex. The two of them hit it off, and my mother told Ivy about Olga and her refusal to let Maya come to stay with them even for a short while. Ivy immediately offered her own living room couch, expressing her utter shock that a family member could be so unwelcoming after so many years of being apart.

A few days later, while still staying among the wolves herself but having secured a temporary place to stay for Maya at the kind and generous neighbor's apartment, my mother went to pick my sister up at the bus station. My poor sister hadn't even have time to settle in to Ivy's apartment before my uncle and aunt started in on her.

"What the heck are you doing here?" my uncle said to Maya as soon as she saw her. "Why are you making problems for everyone?"

"What problems am I making, uncle?" she replied deferentially. "First of all, I called maminka to ask her if I could come, and she said yes. Secondly, we are supposed to be family. Why aren't you happy to see me?"

"My dear, we are in Canada here! No one is going to admire your looks or give you special favors. You can't just waltz in like you own the place! I don't care how pretty you are, here you are *nobody*!" Olga barked at her like a bulldog from the doorway of Ivy's apartment. My sister, tall and lovely as she was, must have inspired especially strong hatred in Olga, who no doubt saw Maya's beauty as a personal affront to her.

My uncle and aunt eventually lost interest in their teasing and unkind words and left Maya and my mother alone. My sister stayed at Ivy's apartment for two days, and then all too soon it was time for her to go back to Montreal and say her goodbyes to the Greek family that had so kindly taken her in during my mother's absence.

I wouldn't see my sister again until a few years after this, since our paths never crossed. I was still in Greece experiencing challenges of my own.

While my mother lived among wolves, I met one of my own.

My life with Manolis back in Greece was as one can expect when one is lost in the world. He tried his best to entertain me. He took me out to the beach a couple of times to help me cope with my feelings, but the poor man had been saddled with much more than he'd bargained for when it came to caring for me. I couldn't sleep at night, I was exhausted all the time, confused about everything that had happened, and just in plain distress. It felt like my life was enveloped in a thick fog, and it was about to become even foggier.

Manolis spoke English so we communicated fine, and he was kind to me—however, in my constant state of confusion and tiredness, I frequently felt the need to leave the small, cluttered, dark apartment in the middle of noisy downtown Athens. People were always shouting and yelling, music from nearly every balcony lingered in your ears, piercing sirens from police vehicles filled the air, ambulances and fire trucks raced by every few minutes, and the stifling carbon dioxide fumes choked my nostrils and throat. I was becoming more and more claustrophobic, and I needed peace and quiet to reevaluate what was going on in my life.

One day I'd had enough and I asked Manolis if he could call my sister's boyfriend at the time—let's just call him The Boy—to see if he could come pick me up as soon as he could. Manolis reluctantly agreed, because even in my state of mind I think Manolis kind of liked having me around for company. Perhaps I reminded him of my mother.

The Boy arrived, and I was quite happy to see him. I recognized him from my sister's pictures that she had shown me while we were in Montreal together. I was just eager to get the heck out of that apartment, craving a change of scenery.

We arrived at the apartment he shared with his parents, who were very welcoming, sweet people. Their noiseless, sparkling-clean abode was in a much more upscale area just outside of Athens. I stayed in this three-story, peach-colored building on top of a steep hill at the foot of a majestic mountain for the next week.

Before it all went sour, I felt like I had gained a brother. It turns out that he was more of a brother from hell.

In the beginning it was very soothing to be there, despite the turmoil of my thoughts and emotions at the time. I was even starting to smile again. His parents were very understanding of my situation, and desperately tried to make me feel as much a part of the family as they possibly could while still respecting my solitude.

Every day, I made my way behind the apartment building to a little path that led me to the foot of the huge mountain. I would walk to the highest point, gazing out to the horizon and finding comfort in the amazing views that surrounded me. The treeless, rugged landscape of the mountaintop took about an hour to get to. Sheepdogs going about their business would come to see me, somehow sensing my loneliness. The stunning view of the sparkling sea further down over the horizon at the outskirts of town felt like a safe haven for me.

As for The Boy, he was kind and gentle to me, and I felt very close to him in a familial way. After all, he was my sister's boyfriend, and how could I even think of sex in my circumstances? I just wanted another soul to hold me, to tell me that everything would be okay. I wanted to be able to trust another human being without being punished for it. In a way, being close to The Boy felt like being close to my sister again, because he was one of the only tenuous connections I had to her during this time. I missed her, even though I didn't know her very well as we'd spent so much time apart. She was so different from me, but I still loved her dearly and didn't know when I would see her again.

The Boy must have gravely misinterpreted my confused state and need for platonic affection as one of flir-
tation and invitation, because he demolished what was
left of my faith in humanity in a single horrible, selfish
act one day in his room.

We were casually lying down on his bed as we sometimes did—like friends or brother and sister, I thought—
conversing about little nothings. All I remember is that
all of a sudden he was on top of me and pulling my pants
halfway down, and just like that, he penetrated me. I
was beside myself with horror. I didn't scream or fight;
I didn't even say "no" because there was no time. It was
over seemingly in an instant. The whole ordeal must have
lasted less than a few minutes.

I couldn't believe it—the person I had blindly trusted with my fragile state had ravaged through me like a
tornado.

I was stunned and paralyzed as he finished and told
me to get up. I felt so much shame—yes, shame—because
in that moment it felt like I'd let this happen *again*. How
could I have not seen this coming? How could I have let
this happen? Why had he done this to me? I had entrusted
this person with my safety, and I thought that he was supposed to take care of me. He was not supposed to use me in
such a dishonorable way. He had torn my spirit to pieces.

I went to bed that day in such confusion. I didn't
sleep at all. What was I to do now? Where would I go? I
couldn't call Manolis because he would have told me to
stay with The Boy's family. There was nothing to do but

lick my wounds, shake it off, protect my mind as best as I could, and go on.

From that day on, I vowed to myself to never be a victim again. I vowed to never be preyed upon again in my life. *I will become the hunter from now on*, I said to myself, and I suppose I did. As my father so eloquently put it nearly a decade later, "You are the Mata Hari of men." I followed in his footsteps in some ways.

The next day, The Boy took me with him into Athens like nothing had happened. I was still feeling broken, but something had changed in me. His actions had altered my personality, and I had suddenly become numb as well as fearless.

"You know that what happened was your fault," he said to me, a cynical note to his voice.

"What?" I asked in pure disbelief. "What happened is that you raped me!" I continued, angry that he was dismissing what he'd done as somehow my fault. *You son of a bitch*, I wanted to say, but I held myself back.

"No, I didn't," he insisted. "And your sister...she must never find out about this."

"Nope, don't worry. I will tell her nothing," I replied, outraged.

I actually intended to tell her, but since I was unsure of what I would say to her about what had happened and how I would say it, I didn't tell her what had happened for many years to come. It was becoming a habit of mine not to say anything about things like this, thinking that it was my fault—it was my fault for following the guy in

Greece when I was nine, it was my fault for entering a men's washroom, it was my fault for entering that construction area in Montreal when I was ten—and this, well...I felt like I should have known better somehow.

I took responsibility for the situation even though I knew very well that he was the one firmly in the wrong. Back then, I was sure that my sister would have blamed me for what had happened. If only I had told her; if only I had had the courage to tell her what a horrible person she fell in love with, but I just couldn't find the courage to do so, so I buried this secret deep inside me and lived with it for years. The regret of carrying this decision to stay silent was compounded by hearing years later that she was told through a mutual friend of theirs that The Boy had "bragged" about raping me to friends.

When I finally did tell my sister what had happened years later over the phone, she couldn't understand why I had stayed quiet. "I wasted years of my life with this man," she said. "Why didn't you just tell me?" But I had nothing for her: no excuse, no valid answer. I knew very well that she was right. I should have told her, but similar horrible experiences in the past had taught me not to say anything for fear of getting blamed for it. How could I have known that my sister would have been on my side and believed me? I didn't yet trust my sister's loyalty at the time. Keeping that secret took a toll on our relationship that was difficult to recover from.

Only a short time after the incident with my sister's boy-friend, I was headed back to Canada to build a new life yet again with my mother. She'd given me the rest of the money she'd gotten from her jewelry after she'd bought her plane ticket back to Canada. Once she had arrived in Toronto and gotten more or less settled, she sent word for me to join her, and I paid for my ticket with the money I'd tucked away for just such an occasion.

I arrived in Toronto completely oblivious to her ordeal with the wolves—but I was about to find out how bad my mother's time in Toronto had been while I was away. I experienced firsthand Olga's inexplicable hatred toward my mother. I saw it in the way she looked at her as well as in her snappishness toward her. We stayed with my uncle and Olga for two days after I had returned from Greece, and then Olga happily found a room for us to rent. There, we began to rebuild our relationship around the seven absent years in each other's lives.

But seven years is a long time in a child's life; I was not the same person, nor was I anything that my mother had expected me to be. To her disappointment, I had inevitably become a mini version of my father due to his influence over me. It took some time for us to understand each other and to see each other with new, accepting eyes, and adaptation was difficult.

I, shockingly, still loved my father. I wanted to keep some type of relationship with him, so I begged my mother not to take him to court for alimony. Because I was not eighteen yet, the courts would have ordered him to pay child support. Reluctantly, in order to keep peace between us, she agreed. She told me that it was her intention to put the alimony payments aside for me so that I would have savings for later on in life, but I didn't see it that way at the time. It took me over a decade to understand all of her decisions from that period once maturity had stepped in.

I still had Stockholm syndrome where my father was concerned, and I didn't really understand how that worked at the time. In a way I did love him; after all, I lived with him for seven years and got used to my peculiar life with him. My mother, in order to make me happy, agreed to just about anything concerning him. I remember defending him at all costs. She must have been in such agony and frustration listening to me. Had I forgotten everything he'd put us through?

But my memories of the deceptive monster that was my father would come back to me little by little, and confusion slowly overwhelmed me as I was pulled between feelings of love and hate for this man. I sometimes deliberately antagonized my mother by being rude to her boyfriend at the time, who would defend me regardless of how I behaved and who always treated me so kindly, probably sensing my confusion. But my mother stood by me through it all, perhaps knowing very well what I was going through, feeling my turmoil, and hoping that one day I would understand her point of view.

We found a really nice apartment in North York, Toronto, right where the 401 and 404 highways meet. It was a nice area; it e-ven had a pool (which I seldom used). I went to school, and little by little, life took on a new shape. My mother and I learned more and more about each other every day, but my resurfacing flashbacks amplified my confusion as well as my love for Caesar.

I disliked living in Toronto throughout the seven years we were there, and I knew that one day I would be back home to Quebec, which I had learned to love and cherish for its particular lifestyle. But until then, I would stay with my precious mother—I needed her in my life. Slowly, she taught me to become a woman, to take care and be proud of myself. She also taught me forgiveness.

She began to work in a Greek restaurant again, and things were going well for us. Unfortunately, this was when reoccurring flashbacks started to raise havoc for me. I was lost, completely lost. I felt like I belonged nowhere—not in Slovakia, not in Greece, not in Toronto, not even in my beloved Quebec. I was homeless, but not in the sense of not having a physical home. I felt empty inside. Not even my dear mother could fill that void.

I began seeing an Italian man, Sal, who was older than me by nearly ten years. I would spend my weekends at his parents' house, and there I terrorized the whole family with my reoccurring nightmares. His brother was petrified of my screams, saying that I sounded like a lost little child.

One respite from these mental tortures was my visits to Greece to see my sister, who had successfully moved back to Athens by this time. My mother sent me nearly every summer, and I was so thankful to be back in my beloved Greece, where I indulged in the sweetness of everything the country had to offer. One year I went camping on my own in a really beautiful area near a forest. My tent was only a few meters from the water, as well, and the nights gave me the perfect view of the bioluminescence in the ocean; microscopic creatures generating enough power to illuminate the rocky shoreline as far as the eye could see. In the evening I would meet travelers from every corner of this wonderful planet and we would talk, laugh, and sing the night away.

I remember feeling fearless as well as curious during this phase of my life. I would stride around confidently with my shoulders back, as if to say, "Don't mess with me." One day, while walking along a winding road in the wooded area behind my campsite, I caught the first glimpse of the next stop on my destiny's path. There it was: Club Med. I hopped the fence and made myself right at home. The place was out of this world. There were bamboo huts everywhere and little pathways amongst the trees leading you to each hut. There was a small volleyball court, and next to it was the tiny, welcoming reception area where the restaurant was. Mainly, it was the staff that intrigued me: young people casually striding along in sarongs with huge smiles on their faces, waving at every single person they passed. I felt like I'd stumbled upon paradise.

No one ever questioned my being there at first. I played volleyball with the GO's (Gentile Organizer), or staff, and the GM's (Gentile Member), or tourists. I helped with activities like volleyball and bingo as well as helped tourists put on their skis for their jet-ski adventures.

About a week later, the chief of the village (that's what the clubs are called, villages) came to see me.

"Hey, we've noticed that you are here quite a bit, but that you don't live here," the chief said to me, shirtless with his sarong slung low around his waist. I'd been caught!

"Yeah, I'm at the campground next door, but I really love it here," I replied, figuring that I might as well tell him the truth. I kept a huge smile on my face, scared that he would throw me out from my new paradise.

"What would you say if I offered you a job?" he asked, completely taking me by surprise.

"What?" I said, gobsmacked. "Wow, I would love to, but I have to go home, school is starting. I'm only here to visit my sister." Of course, I could have said yes, but this was the only answer I could come up with on the spot.

"Okay then," he said with an easy smile. "Let me know if you change your mind. In the meantime, you are more than welcome to stick around. We really enjoy your company." With that, he left me with my new friends.

This experience was like visiting another world, and it awoke the dormant adventure bug that Caesar had instilled in me years ago. I was hooked. Even though I chose not to stay that summer—God knows why—I was going to find a way to travel, even if it took years to accomplish.

And sure enough, years later, my path would lead me back to Club Med—this time in the Dominican Republic. I guess it was my destiny after all.

At school back in Toronto, I was a bit of an outcast with only a few good friends. One of my teachers noticed my unhappiness and took pity on me by trying to help me however he could.

One of my distractions from the trials of my daily life was learning about geography and daydreaming about travel. I had a large atlas at home, and I would avidly scan the pages and memorize all the different places I wanted to visit one day. My teacher found out about my knowledge of and passion for geography and travel, and he put me in charge of teaching a geography class in his absence a couple of times a month. This empowered me as well as helped me to engage and involve myself in my own life, which I'd felt so strangely distant from for so long. I would also help him grade exams, and he always made sure I had important assignments like preparing documents for the class or for field trips in order to keep my mind busy.

I loved this teacher dearly. I am convinced that he was put on my path for the simple reason that he partly accomplished what my mother couldn't. She gave it everything she had, but the seven years we were apart made it difficult for us to see eye to eye on many things and to

truly connect with each other. I think that she was perplexed as to why I wasn't as happy as I should have been,
and she tried desperately to help me in every way she
could imagine. We were both so lost during this time—
reweaving the gap between us was a task that couldn't be
accomplished overnight.

With a little help from Father Time as well as a few
added life experiences under my belt, my mother and I
grew to love and appreciate each other deeply. Eventually,
we become best friends, and I fully grasped the true degree of her sorrows. I believe that having my own children
in my thirties helped me to understand how agonizing it
must have been for her to have her child taken away from
her. I finally understood the meaning of a mother's pure
love for her child.

But all of this came later. First, I had to follow the
siren's call of adventure that my peek inside paradise
had awoken in me. I didn't realize it at the time, but my
yearning for travel was a way of ignoring my Pandora's
Box of unresolved pains and traumas—a box that was
about to be opened.

Part Two

A Road to Healing on Destiny's Path

June 2002

"Why do you have to go to Europe again? You haven't had enough of traveling yet?" my mother asked me, her discontent quite obvious in her tone as we spoke over the phone just a few days before I was going to leave for Italy.

"I don't know, Mami...I just do. Something is calling me there. I need to go and find out what that is," I told her. I truly couldn't explain my sudden urge to go to Italy better than that.

I was 29, and my itch to travel the world refused to be ignored. I was an adult in charge of my own decisions, and I was going regardless of my mother's confusion and discontent.

I arrived at Mirabel airport in Montreal five hours prior to my departure. The check-in was quite speedy, and I felt like this was a good sign that I was on the right track. I was leaving...finally! This trip had a special feeling to it somehow. It was going to be different.

Why did I have this constant hunger for the new, the unknown, and the dangerous? For the thrill of getting myself in and out of exciting predicaments? I didn't know the answers to these questions for a long time; all I knew throughout many of my early adventures was that I yearned for excitement and distraction. I know now that I was living for those things because they gave me an opportunity to busy myself elsewhere instead of facing my demons.

Adventure. It was embedded in my DNA. Was I born with a wandering soul, or had the adventurer in me been born when my father kidnapped me? Regardless of the reasons, my thirst for leaving behind the status quo and looking forward to the unknown was all-consuming. I longed to solely rely on my instincts; to let them guide me in whatever direction they willed and, most importantly, to always keep me a step ahead of facing my past and all the darkness that lurked there.

But there was something different about this trip to Italy. I could sense it. This time, I was leaving for my 30th birthday, and I had begun to become aware of my habit of running from my past. I was hoping to find the path to healing and to make peace with the haunting memories that kept creeping their way into my life no matter how far I ran.

With the bitterness of my conversation with my mother still heavy in my heart, I decided to call an ex of mine, Gigi, one last time before I left. I just wanted to say goodbye, and perhaps to hear him say what I already knew: that this was it. We needed to give each other back our freedom and move on, and it was becoming quite evident to me that I needed to focus on my healing, not on a relationship. I needed to deal with things once and for all and follow the true path of my destiny. Gigi understood this clearly, and that last conversation helped me to close one door so that another could be opened.

The road to this door had been a long and winding one, however.

June 1999

I landed a job as a travel agent in a small travel agency in Trois-Rivières, Quebec, right after graduating from college with two certificates: one as a travel agent and one as a tour guide. I didn't know it at the time, but this decision would help to bring me closer and closer to my destiny.

I had ended up going back to my beloved Quebec after nearly seven years of living in Toronto with my mother. The move happened quite rapidly—it was a spur-of-the-moment kind of decision. I went to visit my father as well as a good friend of mine whom I had left behind when I went to live with my mother in Toronto.

My friend and I went to a neighboring tavern to catch up, and that night I met a guy with whom I really hit it off. I ended up spending the weekend with him, and the next week I called my mother to tell her that I was head over heels in love and that I was moving back to Quebec to live with him. In her pure and devoted love for me, she was happy for me and did not question my impulsive decision.

That relationship, doomed from the beginning, lasted two and a half years. It was near the end of it when I decided to go back to college and get my certificates, my hunger for adventure still brewing in my veins. I ended up going back to live with my father while I finished my studies, which I paid for on my own. I also paid a small portion toward the rent on his apartment, which he shared with his new girlfriend and her two daughters. I studied hard, earned my certificates, and landed the job at the travel agency shortly after.

The travel agency was in a private home on one of the smaller streets of Trois-Rivières, but still close to downtown. The city, with its ghastly smell from the paper mill, became my home for around a year. The house that hosted the agency was an older-style home that was quite cold during the unforgivable Quebec winters. I worked in the front of the home where the agency was located.

Upon entering the home, along the hallway on your left-hand side was a doorway to a large room where the agency was located. On the right-hand side of the hallway was a small storage room with an extra computer, which helped to fill the void of my many lonely evening hours. At the end of the hallway was a door that led to the other half of the house, including a cute little apartment. This apartment became my home—a courtesy of the owner, as I didn't have enough time to find a place of my own, and maybe my subconscious knew that I was not going to stay long in this place. The apartment was quite cute, with a bedroom on the left-hand side, a kitchen that we shared during the day, and a doorway that led you to a city-style back yard that was more of a parking lot than anything else.

The drawback of working at the agency was that I was extremely envious of my clients. They were living my dreams, after all, while I was stuck behind a desk making it happen. However, one of the many perks of working at a travel agency at that time was the Familiarizing Tours, or Fam Tours as we called them in the industry, which didn't cost as much as they do today. We travel agents were encouraged to go on as many Fam Tours as we could. I had the chance to go on two of them, and the tour I took to Mexico was the one that drove me even closer to my destiny.

Fam Tours seemed like mini vacations, but really they weren't. We were sent to one of the destinations that we were promoting in order to familiarize ourselves with what the hotels had to offer so that we could sell our clients the best possible vacation suited to their needs once we came back. These tours were usually between three and five days in length, and we visited five to ten hotels a day. You quickly became confused, since after a while most of them began to look the same. Even with the numerous pictures we all took, it became quite a challenging puzzle to solve when we got back and had to match our selling points with all the hotels we'd seen.

My first three-day Fam Tour, curiously enough, was in Punta Cana, Dominican Republic, where nearly a year later I spent a year experiencing unimaginable adventures as a tour guide working for—you guessed it—Club Med. But it was the tour to the stunning Mexican Riviera Maya that truly revealed my path to me.

Upon arriving at the Cancun airport, I met up with the wonderfully eccentric group of people with whom I would be sharing the tour of the Mexican Riviera Maya, and we were then greeted by our guide. My group consisted of quite a few unusual travel agents also arriving from all over Canada to partake in the fun of spring breakers' paradise. The energy was palpable, and we couldn't wait for our free evenings that came after the daytime tours of countless hotel lobbies, two or three different types of rooms in each, and many different types of restaurants, beaches, spas, fitness rooms, and amazing pools.

Our bus included one of my eccentric co-travelers, a sweet, chubby guy who was always listening to Era, a musical group with beautiful, angelic voices that seemed to transport you to another universe. Another co-traveler was a cute young ladies' man who was there to really take it all in, if you know what I mean. There were also a couple of women in their thirties who were very kind and funny. We had the best of times teasing and laughing with each other.

Fortunately for us, our tours didn't consist of hotel hopping only; we also had the privilege to do some sightseeing. One of our excursions was to Xel-Ha Park, one of the world's largest aquatic theme parks, nestled among the jungle by the sea. Its crystal-clear waters and lagoons transported you to another world, and snorkeling took on a whole new meaning floating through the soft current of the spectacular "lazy" river. Hundreds of different types of fish surrounded you, curious as to what you brought them, some gently poking your toes and others passing you by. A pure joy.

The hotels in the area were situated along spectacular beaches of gorgeous turquoise-blue waters and white sands that felt like baby powder between your toes. You'd frequently smell the enticing scent of BBQ as you swam in one of the uniquely shaped pools, and the engaging salsa music surrounded your whole being, making your feet want to move and your body want to sway to the sweet, sexy melodies. Needless to say, everything about the region made you want to stay there forever. Soon enough, I would be back to this particular slice of paradise...as well as to the other side of this deceiving golden prison.

In one of the more luxurious all-inclusive hotels along the stunning vistas of the Mayan Riviera, I met a manager by the name of Manuel who played an instrumental role in this particular twist in my destiny's road. He was a very handsome man of average height, with dark hair and very attractive, well-kept facial hair. Instant attraction sprang up between us without even a spoken word exchanged. This must have been quite obvious—all of my co-travelers started teasing me about how we only had eyes for each other during the whole presentation at his hotel.

After what seemed an eternity, Manuel ended his speech about the wonders and uniqueness of his hotel, and everyone applauded and spread out for some refreshments around the pool. Shortly after, Manuel approached me, his enchanting cologne making every inch of my body vibrate.

"Hello," he said in his Mexican accent, his piercing brown eyes locking with mine. "How did you enjoy the presentation?"

"It was...very interesting," I said stupidly, as I was having a difficult time forming a complete sentence.

"Would you and your friends like to join me this evening for a drink at the lobby bar?" he asked.

"Yes, of course, I...I mean, we would love to join you. Let's say around eight o'clock?" I managed to reply. He nodded and smiled, and we chitchatted for a while longer before he took his leave

That evening my roommate and I took a long time getting ready in our beautiful hotel room overlooking the turquoise waters below. Our room had that wonderful smell of southern humidity: a mixture of mild mildew, bleach, dampness from the pools and showers, sunbaked sand, and the mist from the sea. It's a smell that transports you to another place in time. The Mexican decorations with their bright reds, yellows, and blues, the terracotta walls, and the beautifully handcrafted clay washroom sinks all made you feel like a queen in her bower, and the atmosphere surrounding made you feel alive and almost disoriented.

Pampered and manicured, we arrived at the hotel lobby. Manuel was already waiting for me at the bar, and he looked oh -so- handsome in his casual green suitpants and a light green shirt open at the collar and rolled at the wrists.

After a few polite greetings with my co-travelers, he turned to me and handed me a beautiful white flower that smelled divine—a sweet mix of vanilla and jasmine. All of my friends were giggling behind him at their bar tables and making silly kissing faces at me. Ignoring their childish but lovable behavior was not hard to do, for I had my chosen prey before me, and soon the sound of their laughter dissipated into the general noise of the busy bar and lobby.

"How are you liking your stay?" Manuel asked.

"Oh it's wonderful," I replied with enthusiasm. "We are so lucky to be staying in such a prestigious hotel. Thank you for having us." I figured that it wouldn't hurt to stroke his ego a bit. After all, it was all true. "I would love to work in a place like this one day," I continued.

"Well, if you are truly interested, I would love to have you work here. I am sure I can find you a position among us. Let me know, yes? Here is my card..." He handed me a small piece of paper, smiling his beautiful smile. "You will find all the information you need on it, so email me whenever you are ready."

"Well, you will get an email from me very soon, because it is my dream to work down south," I said to him with an answering grin, realizing that my dream was getting closer and closer and that a door had just opened up for me.

"I'll be happy to make that dream become a reality," he said, his tone genuine.

When I arrived back at the agency after our trip, the return to day-to-day reality was harsh in more ways than one. I just wanted to give my two weeks' notice and disappear to paradise! But it wasn't my time quite yet, so I readjusted slowly to my solitude as best as I could and distracted myself by surfing the Internet aimlessly for hours. This was not a sustainable plan, however. I had to do *something*—there had to be some movement in my life. This stagnant state was quickly taking a toll on me.

On one of these boring, solitary days, I decided to metaphorically throw a message in a bottle into the ocean and post a very original ad on a dating site. Little did I know that this message was just another footfall on my life's path. My dating blurb said, "I come from a country that didn't make war while separating. Where do I come from?" I had many responses—some not quite as witty as others, and some very interesting indeed—and among them was a man named Gigi. His response caught my eye. It said, "I will get back to you with the correct answer so that I don't look like a fool," but what caught my attention was his signature: a dolphin. As crazy and completely ludicrous as it sounds, I fell in love with this man...over a dolphin. I loved what they represented: an intelligent, gentle yet protective, loving, funny, and playful creature.

I decided to write him back, and it only took a few exchanges before I could "feel" the man behind the screen. It didn't take long for us to want to meet. Before we did, we spent many hours on the phone chatting, and we continued to write back and forth. He would tell me about his many adventures with Club Med as a diving instructor in Turks and Caicos, spending every chance he got diving with Club Med's mascot, Jojo—you guessed it, a dolphin.

I fell in love with Gigi so quickly. There was just something about him; something quite different that I couldn't really put my finger on. He was a special creature, as some would say. Perhaps it was his travels that intrigued me, or his oh-so-radiant, infectious, positive personality that I could never get enough of.

I decided to kill two birds with one stone and meet up with him at a party I'd been invited to in Montreal that was hosted by Nolitour, a travel wholesaler. Nervous and excited, I drove to the cute little pub in Montreal by the waterfront where the party was taking place. When I saw him holding his little girl in his lap, I fell in love with him for real. He looked like a movie star with his handsome shaved head and warm blue eyes—he just emanated positive energy. He introduced me to his daughter and then we spoke for a while, smiling at each other and laughing, reveling in the instant electricity between us that was strong enough to be almost unnerving. He wrote down his address on a piece of paper for me so that I could meet up with him later on that evening after my party. Needless to say, I was quite eager to get the hell out of there.

I was anxious the whole drive over to his house, but also very excited about the new adventures that surely lay ahead. I arrived at his house on the outskirts of Montreal in Laval, which was situated in a beautiful neighborhood filled with beautiful houses next to the river that separated Montreal from Laval. Nearly every house had a pool and an elegant boat at their dock. His house was across from the ones bordering the water.

As soon as I entered his warm and charming Victorian-style home, I was greeted by Spock, a cute little fluffy orange cat who was the house mascot. The house smelled Victorian inside and out—a woody, welcoming odor like that of an antique store—which warmed your soul upon entering. Without taking his eyes off me, Gigi offered me his hand, which I shyly took as he guided me all the way up the bulky wooden stairway toward the upstairs loft.

The loft, which looked more like something you would expect to see in a Mont-Tremblant chalet, had a very imposing rock fireplace in the middle with an array of comfy couches surrounding it and massive wooden beams across the triangular ceiling. Its cozy, dim atmosphere would set the tone for the many romantic nights that we would share over the next year.

The space suited him perfectly. I lay my head down on his lap on the huge couch in front of Her Majesty the fireplace. The flames spoke our language that night. As he caressed my hair, I couldn't conceive that I had to leave in the morning. His touch was tender—so loving and manly at the same time. We did not make love that night, but I had never experienced such feelings before. As corny as it sounds, it was a magical time.

When I came back to the agency, I gave my two weeks' notice.

I packed my bags, left my job, and started my wonderful, passionate, crazy love affair with this man—jobless and with empty pockets as I was. It lasted for less than one year. We literally lived from love and water, as the saying goes. I got a part-time job as a hostess in addition to helping him with his odd jobs as an entertainer for special parties as well as a decorator for malls on holidays. I even had the chance to organize a boxing event for the famous boxer Arturo Gatti, which I am extremely proud of to this day.

We didn't lead an ordinary life, but the experiences we had together were out of this world. We had incredible sexual chemistry, and everywhere we went people seemed to be mesmerized by our energy. We spent our summer days around the huge sheltered pool at his home, afloat in our own universe. As the new millennium dawned, we lay intertwined up in his loft—the New Year's night belonged to us, and we didn't want to share it with anyone.

Unfortunately, my unresolved childhood issues eventually came out to play in our seemingly carefree relationship. As I mentioned earlier, he had a six-year-old little girl. In the beginning everything was fine, as the two of us were still living in a state of pure euphoric passion. However, it didn't take long for my uneasiness to surface whenever his daughter would visit. I realized after a while that it was not the little girl's visits that were the problem—it was my traumatic past catching up to me once again.

Noticing and watching Gigi being so tender, loving, understanding, playful and funny with his daughter was pure torture for my heart, which still felt like the heart of a little girl in many ways. I needed healing, but instead I evaded by plunging myself into our love affair. I was still avoiding opening my Pandora's Box, too afraid of what would come out. I hid these profound and frightening feelings very deep, thinking that they would just go away on their own. I didn't realize at the time that, if I never faced what was in that box, I would never be free. Because of this, I was living a strained and unfulfilling life despite my happiness with Gigi.

Whenever his little girl visited, feelings emerged in me that I understood nothing about—I wouldn't understand these feelings until much later on in my life. My childish and unpredictable reaction toward her was one of pure jealousy; I didn't want to share him with anyone, not even his own daughter, even though he seldom got the chance to see her. I didn't understand why my poor heart ached so fiercely whenever she was around. I felt like we were in competition for his affection. I felt like I was the one who needed his touch, his warm words, and his unconditional love the most, not realizing that I was wishing for those things from my own father but projecting it onto him and his relationship with his daughter.

But the poor girl needed her father's love more than I did, and I was in her way, so she reacted like any six-year-old child would: with resentment and good, old-fashioned temper tantrums. It was unbearable—I couldn't stand it. My past was creeping up on me like Nova Scotia's fog, deep and thick, but still I didn't want to face things. I refused to see that I had unresolved issues, and even though I thought I was perfectly happy, those issues prevented me from living my life to its full potential for longer than I care to admit.

For a while I wanted to leave—somewhere, anywhere—and I wanted him to go with me, but I knew very well that he would not leave his daughter behind. How could he? He wanted to be there for her, like the sweet, caring, silly father that he was; a father that I would have loved to have had when I was a little girl.

Needless to say, even though we had a passionate love that I cherished, things like my desire to see the world, my yearning for adventure, our age difference, and the conflicting emotions that his little girl's presence brought up in me eventually took a final toll on the relationship. We said our painful goodbyes after not even a whole year together, and I moved out to a friend's house.

Gigi was and still is a big part of my life. He is a very unique individual who does not fit in with society's idea of "normal." He is a very spiritual and positive person and an eccentric life coach who was once a lost soul himself for a while. He is a wonderful person who is extremely likable, warm, loving, and a pleasure to be around. It was a terrible experience to say goodbye to a man who had loved me like no other and gave me so much more than I thought I deserved, but I am also grateful that we have remained friends.

Escaping Reality through Adventure

Mexico, Fall of 2000

Not even a month had passed after my break-up with
Gigi when I decided it was finally time to make the call to
Mexico. It had been approximately a year, after all, and I
didn't want to let the chance slip by entirely.

"Hi, Manuel, it's C.C.," I said into the phone, hearing both my nervousness and my excitement in my voice.
"Remember me?" We had kept in touch throughout that
period with emails, and he'd continued to make it perfectly clear that, whenever I was ready, he would arrange
everything.

"Yes, of course!" he replied with the same enthusiasm. "You are ready now? Are you really sure?"

"Yes I am—more than you know. How do we make it
happen? I'm ready whenever you want me down there," I
said.

"Okay, well let me make some arrangements and I will call you as soon as I can, alright? Hang in there, and I will talk to you very soon with all the details."

I told him that I'd be waiting patiently and that I'd talk with him soon, and hung up with a knot of anticipation in my throat. I felt absolutely fearless; it never crossed my mind the dangers that Mexico might pose. All that mattered was that I was finally leaving.

You know that you are on the right track when what you've most been wishing for becomes a reality almost effortlessly. Manuel called me not even two days later with great news.

"Hi C.C.," he said. "I hope you're still interested, because I've arranged for you to be picked up at the Cancun airport in two weeks. There will be a chauffeur waiting for you. I am sending you all the details in your email."

"Of course I'm still interested!" I said, barely able to contain myself. "I can't wait to get there and be a part of your team. Manuel, I can't thank you enough. I'll see you soon". As he was giving me the details of my flight number, it took every ounce of control from me not to scream and jump up and down with pure joy.

I was all packed up by the next day, and the rest of the week was an agony of counting down the hours, which were not going by nearly quickly enough. It felt like my dream was just out of arms' reach. I had no idea what awaited me, but I was ready for it nonetheless.

It was late October of 2000 when I arrived in the small Cancun airport on a warm fall evening. As Manuel promised, there was a chauffeur waiting for me with my name on a white tablet, which he was holding high up over his head. He greeted me politely but slightly coldly, and then he helped me with my army-style bag to the taxi. We drove silently to the prestigious hotel of Bahia Principe Tulum, where Manuel was waiting for me. I was still amazed at how smoothly everything had panned out—it felt right. Of course, I was so full of hope and excitement that I failed to see that I was viewing my new adventure through rose-tinted glasses, and not considering the possibility of disappointment that lurked around the corner.

As we entered through the heavy, elegant gate of the hotel, my taxi driver announced my arrival to the front desk. The huge, sophisticated, and tastefully decorated hotel remained the same as I remembered.

"Good evening, C.C.," Manuel said as he approached, "and welcome to Mexico and your new home! Did you have a nice flight? Are you tired? Would you like something to eat before I take you to your room?" His demeanor was very professional; completely different than the one I remembered. I told him thank you but no, I wasn't really hungry and I would rather get my things ready for tomorrow. I was a little bit surprised by his new behavior. I didn't know what to expect, really—perhaps I'd been thinking of the full red-carpet treatment.

"Okay, let me take you to your room, then. Tomorrow morning, come to my office and I will give you the official tour and introduce you to your new colleagues." With that, he brought me to my room and I proceeded to get settled in.

My room was exactly as I expected it to be. It had that wonderful, familiar smell of humidity that I adored. I was happy to have my own room...for now, anyway.

I didn't really sleep well that night with all the anticipation racing through my mind and veins. The next day I was introduced to the staff and to my new position as receptionist. My heart sank, but again, I wasn't sure what I was expecting—Manuel and I never made concrete plans about what position I was to take once I arrived, since I'd only asked him to get me there at any cost.

Unfortunately, I wasn't too excited about my new position at the elegant reception area, which everyone seemed to covet except for me. I didn't really fit in; it felt too serious, and at the time I just wanted to bathe in my new exotic surroundings and have fun, which was in short supply at my desk. All I could think about was how much fun the animation team looked like they were having, and that I wanted to be part of it.

"Manuel, can I talk to you?" I said to him not even a week after my arrival.

"Yes of course, C.C., what's on your mind?" he asked inquisitively.

"I am so grateful for everything you have done for me—I hope that you know that—but I was wondering if I could be a part of the animation team instead of working at reception? I'm just not enjoying myself at reception, and frankly I don't think I'm that good at it. Do you think you could do me a favor and switch me over?" I felt ashamed to be asking him for a favor so soon after my arrival, but he considered what I'd said and seemed to be fine with my request.

"Well, C.C., I can see that you are not enjoying yourself up here at the desk...are you sure that this is what you want?" he asked, his brows furrowing. "You know that if you go with the animation team, you will be downgraded, in a sense. You will lose some privileges, and you will be living with four people in the same room in a little place that's a bus ride away. Is this what you were thinking of when you left Canada? You are lucky to have this position, but if this is what you truly want, I can make it happen." He seemed disappointed, but he clearly wanted to be accommodating, as well.

"Yes Manuel, I am sure," I said, and he smiled at me. "I want to do something that I cannot do in Canada; I can always find a job at hotel reception, but I want to experience things here that I can't back home."

The next day I was packed and ready to move in with my new crazy team with absolutely no regrets.

The animation team members with whom I would be living greeted me with such love and affection that I felt at home right away. Our tiny apartments were about a fifteen-minute drive from the hotel in a tiny village called Chemuyil, located in the thick jungle. This was where all the action happened. There seemed to always be a party going on somewhere. I was the only foreigner on the team—everyone else was Latino, and they wondered aloud as to why in the hell I wanted to join them and take a substantial decrease in salary in order to have this job, but they accepted me nonetheless. I became a sort of sweet, goofy mascot for the team, since I was the odd one out. I paired up with two girls from the Dominican Republic, Maribel and Beatrice, in our tiny room. Boy were they messy, but still fun.

The job was exactly what I wanted it to be. We "played" all day long with the guests, making sure their expectations were met and that they were having a fantastic time on their vacation. Our days consisted of playing bingo by the pool, conducting salsa dancing lessons, playing volleyball at the beach, and all sorts of other activities from nine a.m. until two o'clock in the morning. We had to devote our utmost attention to the guests and their experience—exactly what you would expect in an all-inclusive resort, in other words.

Our days were so packed that it took me a whole week to feel the ocean water on my feet. Yet even surrounded by paradise, I realized that I didn't truly belong here either, somehow—I liked my new position, but I was still desperately searching for a place of my own in the world. How could I have been so miserable in this Eden? I still didn't want to deal with my box of repressed memories and emotions that I kept hidden away inside of myself, and so these feelings of restlessness and unfulfilled desires persisted. I felt like I had to keep moving, because if I stayed still for too long, I knew that everything would swim to the surface and I'd be forced to face it. But for now, I just wanted to continue to float along in the tides of my life with ease, even if I still felt restless.

My Spanish at the time was non-existent, and the first thing I learned to say was "como se dice," which means "how do you say...?" Since I knew three other languages, French, Slovak, and Greek, it didn't take me long to learn Spanish—in three weeks I became quite fluent with a little help from my best buddies Raul, Hector, and Gery. Once, they took me for a movie night in Cancun, where we saw two movies and ate tacos from a young street vendor who couldn't have been older than eleven.

One day, Gery, a cute, short little guy with a quite substantial head of hair, asked me if I wanted to go with them to Playa Del Carmen, a little tourist village about 40 kilometers away from the hotel to meet up with a friend of his at one of the bars by the beach. The adventurer in me was always up for anything that life had to offer, and I said yes. Little did I know that this decision was to take my adventures to a whole new level.

We drove for about 30 minutes from the hotel to Playa Del Carmen in a beat-up old car; six people singing and dancing in our seats while sipping on cheap tequila (very safe, I know). The village was really tiny. We ended up in one of the more distinctive bars on the beach behind the Quinta Avenida, or Fifth Avenue, where all the action took place and where all the tourists gathered. Bars, restaurants, and small shops where everyone wanted you to buy something plus all the nightlife you could possibly need made this little town's atmosphere delightful.

The bar we went to was beautifully decorated with lanterns and traditional bright Mexican colors, and the open patio was awash in animated salsa music. Jovial, enthusiastic, happy people—young and old and from all over the world—surrounded us, many dancing to the captivating rhythm. The bar's lights illuminated the beach, and you could make out a few people sitting on the edge of the crystal-clear water and some swimming out a bit further, away from wondering eyes, to kiss and caress in the gentle waves.

We sat down at a table near the beach, where it turns out that destiny was waiting for me yet again. I never thought the evening would have ended up how it did.

"Hola, Qué onda, güey? Esta hermana es C.C.," (Hey, what's up my man? This sista is C.C.) My friend said affectionately to the guy already sitting at the table while giving him a boyish hug.

"Hi, I'm C.C.," I said while shaking the man's hand. I felt like something was about to change, and quickly. What, I wasn't sure.

"Hi, I'm Gus," he answered with a shy smile. Gus was Mexican, from the city, quite fair skinned, and had beaming light-blue eyes and sun-washed golden hair. He wore tiny round glasses over his slim nose. I trusted him immediately. "So you're working with my friend at the hotel? How do you like it?" he asked with interest.

"It's nice for now," I said, answering his shy smile with one of my own. "I love my boys, but I'm not sure what exactly I want to do next." I reached out and messed up one of my friend's hair amicably. The rest of the gang spread out by then, leaving me to chat with Gus.

"I'm ready for anything really," I continued. "I want to do things, see things, and go places. I don't know how much longer I can take it at the hotel...it's not really what I expected. I might just travel around here!"

"Well, I live in a little apartment here in Playa, close by. You are more than welcome to come over whenever you want with no strings attached, and I can show you around. Just let my friend know and I can pick you up from the hotel. And if you really want, I could sure use someone at the diving shop—"

"Diving shop?" I interrupted, unable to help myself. "I just finished a course in Montreal, but I still have to make a dive to get my certificate. Oh, how I'd love to dive here... Gus, if you're serious, I might take you up on your offer."

My friend Gery came back just then, letting me know that he would not be returning to the hotel since he'd met a girl, and if I wanted to, I could spend the night at Gus's place. He said he trusted his friend, and that I had nothing to worry about. I trusted Gery, and I believed him when he said that I would be safe with Gus.

I looked at Gus, who nodded and said that he was quite happy to have a temporary roommate. We finished our drinks, and then, his blue eyes sparkling, he informed me that we were leaving.

"I want to take you to a special place in the jungle," he told me, excitement clear in his voice.

"Okay..." I answered, puzzled.

"Just trust me, it's magical," he said, squeezing my hand in a reassuring way.

We left the bar and walked through the vibrantly lit streets to his car. On the way, an American and two Mexicans were showing off enormous boas crawling all over them and on the ground. The American walked straight toward me and placed a five-meter albino boa on my shoulders. I froze, my heart pounding wildly in my chest, but the slithering creature just peacefully draped herself along my shaking shoulders, somehow calming me with her own lazy demeanor. I stood there, gently stroking this beautiful, powerful animal whose skin felt both smooth and scaly, cool to the touch. I glanced at the American, letting him know that it was someone else's turn. He gently took her off me, and I was amazed at how calm the creature remained among all of the commotion that surrounded her, with lively tourists passing by as well as pounding music from every corner.

We drove for about a half an hour through the wild jungle, and eventually a remote cave greeted us, candles scattered on each step leading to the entrance, glowing through the blackness of the night. We parked the car and were immediately welcomed by the cave's guardians: flying bats from every direction swooping and hovering over our heads. We walked along the illuminated rocky stairway, which took us deep inside the cave. There, the sound of the silence warmed your soul. This type of silence does have a sound—it is the sound of the whispering vibrations of your own heart. I was completely mesmerized.

We stayed at the end of the cave with only those tiny candles for light for two hours. We meditated, contemplated, and whispered our conversations as to not disturb the Mayan spirits. The sound of the jungle rain slowly permeated through the depth of cavern. It was an out of this world experience.

We left the magical cavern through the wilds of the jungle, and he took me to his apartment in a quieter area of Playa Del Carmen. The apartment was very cute, situated at the end of a remote road a couple of streets behind the hullabaloo of the lively, crowded area we'd spent time in earlier. He was on the second floor of a beautiful two-story white house with a wooden balcony surrounding it. There was a little kitchenette, a nicely sized living room, and quite a large bedroom.

He offered me his futon in his living room. I made sure to tell him about Gigi, whom I was not totally over yet, while we were still in the cave. I was completely captivated by Gus, and I wanted to see where this road would lead. I did somewhat enjoy my job at the hotel, but I still felt a little out of place somehow. I wondered what the heck I was doing there at the resort in my late twenties when most of them were teenagers or only slightly older, but still my desire for adventure grew stronger by the minute. I yearned for excitement more and more, and wasn't yet ready to question what that yearning really meant.

Two days later I was in Manuel's office again, tendering him my resignation. I spoke with total embarrassment and voiced all the apologies I felt were due from someone in my position toward someone who had brought me here in pursuit of my dreams essentially out of the kindness of his heart. But he too was part of my destiny's path, and I thanked him for all he had done for me and told him to keep my last paycheck for his troubles. He refused, and told me that I could always count on him if I got into any trouble. I never did get into any trouble, thankfully, but I did go visit him a few months later; it was the least that I could do.

I stayed with my good friend Gus for a few months after I quit the hotel, and during this time I experienced some of the richest moments of my life. He was always a true gentleman who gave me the opportunity to do things that I would have never have had the chance to do had I not taken the road presented to me on that day in the bar with my friends.

About a week later, Gus informed me that I had to practice my climbing skills (I had none at the time), and that he was taking me on a cenote dive in the heart of the jungle. Cenotes are all over the Yucatan—sinkholes that create caves throughout the Riviera Maya's underground river systems. The name itself means "Mayan river." He also told me that he had discovered this particular precious cave six years ago, in Punta Laguna, where locals had notified him about a hole in the ground with water in it. No one ventured to see what was inside but him. He was slated to take a couple of Germans to the site the next day who were writing an article about it.

That evening, we practiced repelling down his apartment building walls with ropes tied up all around us and attached to the wooden beams on the outside of the building. The neighbors must have thought we were completely insane. I got the hang of it quite fast, and I was ready for the next day with a little added confidence.

We picked up the Germans, Matias and Manuela, at the dive shop and drove deep into the jungle for two hours toward Punta Laguna. When we arrived, we could see the villagers milling around waiting for us. The extreme heat, suffocating humidity, and ferocious mosquitoes made for quite an inviting welcoming committee.

Gus put on his wetsuit, put the tanks on his back, picked up the bag filled with gear and supplies with the help of his coworker, and then we all walked for about 70 meters into the depth of the jungle.

The heat was intolerable when we finally arrived at the exposed hole in the ground, which was surrounded by a homemade security enclosure. Gus informed me that this was the place where we would be repelling down, but not before the Germans had the chance to go down first. My nerves were boiling in my veins, but I was in pure ecstasy—so exciting!

While his coworker helped the Germans descend into the mysterious hole, we went a few meters further into the jungle to the edge of a tiny lake inhabited by a few crocodiles; thankfully, I never had the pleasure of meeting them myself. While we were in front of the tiny lake with its invisible, lurking crocs, Gus saw that I was very keyed up and tried to calm me down.

"C.C., don't be afraid. Okay? I will attach the rope to you, and my friend will help you down. You can't panic once you are in the water, and you can't touch anything, okay? You have to keep calm. I will be waiting for you inside," he said calmly and quietly, trying to extinguish any fear in me. But what he had interpreted as fear about the cave was actually my barely contained glee mixed with my apprehension about the crocs.

"Afraid? Why would I be afraid?" I asked, trying to mask the concoction of excitement and a tinge of almost panic in my voice while eyeing the tiny lake, thinking that at any moment one of its occupants might mistake me for his meal.

"Okay, well, there's also a surprise for you waiting in there. I don't want to tell you what—you will understand why once you get to the water below. Trust me. It will be worth it," he told me while making me practice my newly acquired roping skills.

I trusted this sweet, boyish man; I really did, even if it meant repelling down into a fifty-foot-deep cave in the middle of the jungle with not a soul knowing my whereabouts except for Gus and the two German men.

"Okay, let's do this!" the adventurer in me replied. We made our way back to the hole where we saw the Germans back up at the rim of the cave. They had finished taking pictures in the inside and were now snapping pictures of the surrounding area. Manuela loaned me her wetsuit; it was cold in the cave, she said, without divulging any more information, since Gus had told them not to tell me anything.

"You know how to dive, right?" she asked me warily.

"What? Of course I do. I'm nearly a pro," I reassured her, lying effortlessly and perhaps a little foolishly.

We lowered both of our gear packs down first, and then Gus went down, smiling at me with anticipation in his eyes as he slowly disappeared into the abyss. It was my turn next. My heart pounding, Gus's friend helped me with the ropes, and just like that, he told me to let go of the branch that I was holding onto for dear life. I let go, and I slowly descended into the cave.

There I was, dangling about seventy feet up in the air inside the vastness. The hole in the ground leading to the cenote was small, but the cavity inside was enormous. The cute little bats greeted me by flying all around me. While I was slowly descending toward the water where Gus was waiting for me, I let myself admire the sheer hugeness, my heart still thumping away in my chest. The fusion between the crystalline water and the tiny amount of the sun's rays that penetrated the cavity created beautiful reflections resembling millions of sparkling diamonds. It was one of the most intriguing, superb things I had ever seen. There was also a deep, melancholy feeling to the cavern, almost like the somberness of death, in which the powerful and rich past remained palpable.

I finally reached the water, where Gus untied me from the rope. He then put the tanks on my back, looked straight into my eyes with pure calm and reassurance, told me to put on my mask, gently placed the regulator in my mouth, gave me the universal "okay" sign with his fingers and gently pulled me into the water by the hand.

When I plunged my head in the spectacular, crystal-clear pools of the famous Riviera Maya underground cave systems in this hole in the middle of the jungle, my heart came to a standstill at what I saw. Hundreds of bones, skeletons, and artifacts rested on the pool floor beneath us. We gently and effortlessly floated amongst these ancient remains, and I wondered who they had been and how they'd ended up down here. I tried not to touch anything, afraid of disturbing their souls as well as wanting to respect the enormity and significance of my surroundings. I was humbled. Gus and the documentary people speculated that there could be one or two reasons for the remains in this particular location: they had either been thrown down there for sacrifice, or they had committed suicide.

I was speechless when I came back up. Gus, proud of himself for being a part of something so special in my life, was beaming. I was hooked! I was in a total trance when we left to go back to the apartment.

━ ～

"Good morning, C.C.," Gus said to me one day shortly after our cave expedition, setting a plate of breakfast next to my futon at his apartment. "You need to pack a small bag of your things, for we are going to Mahahual to see a friend of mine there."

Thanking him for the breakfast, I asked how long we would be staying while taking a bite from the fruit salad he had concocted for me. He was so thoughtful.

"Only a couple of days," he replied, a big smile on his face.

After breakfast, he gave me my chores to do for the day. I had to find a *vulcanisador*, or a place where they change tires, so that we would have a safe three-and-a-half-hour road trip. He also made me a list of things to buy at the local supermarket.

I went shopping for our supplies in the tiny store, where I was surprised but delighted by the array of strange-to-me but delicious foods to choose from. I was taking a "bite into life," like Gigi used to say. With all of our supplies ready and packed, we left Playa for the lengthy 286-kilometer road trip.

We drove along the 307 highway and on into the thick jungle to get to Mahahual, where short, stocky Mexican soldiers manning two army stations greeted us. These soldiers, whose job it was to question every person entering the area, were not the most sympathetic people I have ever come across—they were quite scary-looking, actually. Since drug lords used the surrounding waters to move their product from Columbia to their dealers, the area was heavily guarded.

At the time, Mahahual was quite a vacant place without many visitors and with only a couple of streets. This gave the area a remote, sleepy feeling. Once we arrived, Gus's friend Luca greeted us—surprisingly enough—with some vodka, but it was quite nice to have refreshments after such a lengthy and slightly stressful drive. Luca had a cute little house by the long, white, sandy beach where shadows of seaweed inside the turquoise waves cast an uneasy, mysterious mood on the surroundings. We found a spot under a large palm tree right on the beach and set up our tents.

Some meat was roasting away happily over a fire close by; the delicious smell made our stomachs growl. Gus's friend had also prepared some amazing homemade salsa as well as tortillas, which were warming on a plate over the fire. We lay around in the hammocks hanging from the tiny, square-shaped palapas—small beachside dwellings with thatched roofs—while sipping on our refreshments and eating Luca's wonderful food. There were quite a few huge, leafless trees along the beach as well, which added to the slightly lonely and isolated feel to the place. Luca had informed us that we had to snuff out the fire before the sunset as to not attract any "unwanted attention." We did what he asked, and went to bed.

Due to my uneasiness with my new surroundings, I barely slept that night. The morning finally arrived and I could breathe again, my fear of the sounds from the drug lords' boat engines out on the sea throughout the night having made me very anxious. We heard Lucas's salutation of "good morning" and wandered over to the fire. He was cooking again—preparing an extremely spicy omelet that was delicious nonetheless. We ate, and then I met Maria, Gus's ex-girlfriend, who had arrived for a visit as well. She was a sweet person, and she never let her jealousy—if she had any in the first place—be known. Together we went for a little walk further down the mostly barren beach, where I gathered various shells for my collection despite the stark surroundings.

When we came back, Luca was over the fire one last time, cooking us our farewell lunch; the delicious meat again. We ate and thanked him gratefully for his hospitality, packed up our tents, and were on our way back to Playa. The soldiers stopped us on our way back through the checkpoint, gave our car a cursory examination, and let us go through without a hitch. It was quite an unnerving adventure all told. Not my favorite memory, but sometimes it is when you are in close proximity to danger that you feel the most alive.

Recognizing my newfound love of diving, Gus surprised me with an ocean dive after a few weeks after our visit to Mahahual. This time, we dove between Playa and Cozumel, close to where one of the world's most famous diving attractions was located. We packed our gear, and off we went on another adventure. A small boat took us close to Cozumel. I had a grin on my face that said it all—I was in pure heaven, letting myself be transported down my own trail that I had chosen. I wanted to take everything in, to love life, to do exciting things, and let myself flow along the path destined just for me like a leaf on a river's current.

We arrived at our destination, put on our gear, and entered the refreshing, transparent water. I had learned nearly everything I needed to know about decompression as well as times you can stay at certain depths through my diving course in Montreal, but I surrendered myself into the capable hands of my good friend Gus this time, since I didn't feel mentally equipped to be burdened with such a responsibility just yet.

He told me about narcosis; a sensation that I would soon experience. Narcosis is the feeling you get when you reach a certain depth in the water and suddenly have urges to do crazy things, like take off your regulator or mask. Many have drowned this way, so I am glad that I was made aware of it beforehand. I was also glad that I had Gus on my side to guide me through.

Words cannot describe the magic I felt when I was hovering in the water. I felt like I was flying, floating weightlessly in a vast blue quiet where only the *shhhhhh* sound of the air exiting the regulator could be heard. My vision, slightly blurred by the steam inside my goggles, still bore witness to the beauty unfolding before me. Hundreds of different species of fish surrounded us—menacing barracudas coming way too close for comfort with their elongated bodies and a head filled with razor-sharp, intimidating teeth, gracious sea turtles gently soaring along next to and above us—and all around us was the vastness of the turquoise-blue water. It was a pure delight to experience.

The one thing I remember the clearest was the total peace I felt being there. I was floating at around 20 meters, and it looked like there was at least a hundred meters to go below me. We saw a few divers about 40 meters below us, close to the rich, multicolored corals; they seemed so far away in the spectacular immensity of the surrounding sea. I could have died right there and then and I would have been the happiest person on the face of the planet, basking in this sense of unimaginable peace surrounding my whole body.

Gus took me down to 35 meters, and that was when the diving experience gave way to a whole new level of euphoria. I felt like I was drugged—not the bad kind you hear about in the news, but another kind of drug, a happy drug, a life-drug. This high was from another universe. I had a smile on my face from ear to ear and I felt like laughing aloud. Somehow I understood what was going on: I was in a state of pure narcosis.

Gus had stayed floating several feet above me while still holding on to me, watching my every move. He gave me the universal "okay" sign, which I presented right back to him—possibly a bit overly joyful, because he immediately pulled me back up toward him. To my dismay, the feeling subsided right away. I was devastated to have such intense euphoria disappear just like that, and wanted it back. I gestured "you take me down again?" with my hands, and to my surprise and delight, he did, and I was right back in heaven.

I didn't want to ever leave. *Just let me stay here for the rest of my life*, I thought, fully absorbed in my delusional state. He pulled me back up once again after a short while, letting me know it was time to go—we had been diving for three hours, after all. We made our way upward and decompressed, still watching the magnificent depths under our floating bodies. We then surfaced, gave our gear to Gus's coworker on the boat, and hopped inside.

No one talked to each other on the boat ride back to the dive shop; Gus let me enjoy my state of mind, knowing very well how I felt. For the rest of the day, Gus and I spoke only with our eyes. I was in another world inside my head, and when the evening came, on the beach around the fire with his buddies, I desperately wanted to stay clear of the happy crowd while gazing toward the spot where he had taken me just hours ago. Gus made sure to check up on me, bringing me a barbequed lobster that his friend had fished out while we were diving. He stayed by my side while I ate, still silent.

"So, I guess you liked it?" he asked, a small smile on his face.

"Liked it, Gus?" I breathed, the sound of my own voice strange in my ears. "There are no words to describe how I feel right now, and how grateful I am that you took me there, and how glad I am that you offered to let me stay with you, and how happy I am that you are so kind to me. I want to do this every day." I had tears running down my cheeks at this point, which he gently swept away.

"You are on a really big high right now, C.C. It will go away in a couple of days. I am very happy that you liked it," he said, putting his arm around my shoulders. We sat this way on the white, sandy beach in front of the sublime ocean for about an hour, just staring at the water while listening to Mana, a very popular band at the time. There are no words to describe the peace in my heart in that moment.

About a week later, we were out on one of Gus's excursions to a Cenote. The drive was not too long, since Cenotes are everywhere in the area. Inside the muggy, suffocating jungle was a rocky opening that housed an inviting, crystal-blue gateway. This pool led the way to a web of caverns. We passed through tiny holes in the rock inside the transparent water where only our bodies and the rope to which we were tied could fit through. We would go from one opening to another, onwards through the abyss of these entangled caves.

Since the water was so transparent, it felt like we were floating through the air. We surfaced within small cavities inside the labyrinth of Cenotes where only the echoing sound of tiny droplets and our whispers could be heard. I understood then why Gus had warned me not to panic; there was absolutely no way out, and you really needed to stay calm in order to reemerge from the Cenote safely. Although it was beautiful, it was also very claustrophobic.

I never had the chance to dive again, because about week later I received an email letting me know that I would soon have a visitor. My time with my good friend Gus was coming to an end. In the roughly few months I spent in his company, we had found a pleasant rhythm with each other. I helped him to create his new logo for his company, and showed him how to efficiently organize his papers. We even went to Cancun together on several occasions, and enjoyed witnessing the spring breakers reveling at the enormous disco bars.

We really enjoyed each other's company, but my past—in spite of all these wonderful experiences I'd had with Gus—suddenly crept back up on me in the form of Gigi getting back in touch. I realized that this part of me was still calling, and that this life with Gus was not where I was supposed to stay forever.

I told Gus that I would see him soon, but that I needed to see where my feelings lay with Gigi, who had just arrived at the Cancun airport on a cool evening in late fall. I picked him up, and we basically picked up where we had left off. We found each other a beautiful, exotic place to stay near the archeological ruins of Tulum right next to the sapphire ocean. It was a rustic area in the forest with 1970s décor and a tiny outside eating area where the host and owner—a handsome Mexican man—would cook for his guests under a quaint, medium-sized palapa.

Our quarters were of the same style except closed off instead of open. Nearly all of the huts were right by the ocean. Our modest abode had no floor except for the sand from the beach. A wooden bed suspended by ropes swung from the tiny wooden structure's ceiling. Our bed

was surrounded by a white net, and little hermit crabs
made tiny highways in the sandy floor at night, which we
discovered upon waking. Gigi and I swam in the refreshing ocean every morning—an ocean where the spirits of
the ancient Mayans still remained and could be felt in
our souls.

It was the perfect backdrop for our recently re-
vived love affair—an affair that would bring me back to
Montreal just two short weeks later. I went to see Gus
before I left, who, although sad about me leaving, was
supportive of my decision. This little man with his infectious, boyish charm was one of the best things that
had ever happened to me yet, and I was sad to leave him
as well. He had opened doors to me that I'd never even
dreamed of opening, propelling me further along my
life's complex path. He tried to warn me that it was because of my enchanted surroundings that my feelings
were all messed up, but because I wasn't thinking clearly
for that very reason, I didn't see it that way. Riding the
high of my beautiful beachside reunion with Gigi, I followed him back to Canada.

Boy, was Gus ever right—it didn't take long after our
arrival in Montreal in 2001 for the restlessness and regret to settle in. Lying with Gigi in his loft, everything
should have felt like it used to, but how I actually felt this
time couldn't have been further from my memories. My
whole being was screaming, "Get the hell out of here,
you've made a huge mistake!"

My journey was not finished yet, but my feelings for the man beside me who had loved me dearly were. My time in the land of the Mayas was not done yet, either, because two years later, I ended up returning. But first, my path called me elsewhere still.

Florida, spring of 2001

*I*n the spring of 2001, I decided to head to Florida. I was still avoiding dealing with my internal turmoil, and was feeling stagnant with my current situation. I thought about my deep fondness for dolphins often, so I decided to try to get a job working with these wonderful mammals. And so, with $145 in my pocket, I arrived in Florida. My cousin, who had fashioned herself quite a successful life as a caterer, was waiting for me. Her massive, two-story house in a fancy area of West Palm Beach was absolutely gorgeous.

We caught up on life for a couple of days; she was a perky, sweet little thing and I had a lot of fun with her. She loaned me one of her cars to take to the beach whenever I wanted. On one of these beach days, I met two firefighters who informed me that they were going to the Florida Keys. After some chitchat in which I expressed my love for dolphins as well as my wish to work in one of the many sanctuaries for marine life throughout the Keys, they asked me if I wanted to join them. Again, the adventurer in me shouted *yes*.

I told my cousin the good news when I came back from the beach, and she somehow didn't seem to share my enthusiasm. She called the young men, who had given me their phone numbers, in order to obtain additional information to support their case. They arrived the next day, and my cousin took their pictures as well as made a lengthy examination of their driver's licenses. They were very understanding and good-natured about all of this, assuring my cousin that they only had good intentions toward me. After my cousin was satisfied where my safety was concerned, the three of us drove to the Keys.

We drove through the Keys, which are a marvelous chain of tiny tropical islands between the Gulf of Mexico and the Atlantic Ocean connected by long, elegant bridges. A very famous fishing industry arose in this area because of the wide variety of fish that frequent the waters, and the Keys are also a perfect place to scuba dive. We drove from island to island, passing through countless dolphin sanctuaries where my delusions of working for one were quickly cleared away. Every single one of them employed highly qualified volunteers who all had the appropriate degrees in their field, and there I was, degreeless and inexperienced, looking at the world through my rose-colored glasses and living in a hopeful fantasy world.

I was brought back to reality quite abruptly, but without any hint of discouragement. The young men I was traveling with thought I was hurt by my shattered dreams and tried to make me feel better with kind words, but I reassured them that I was perfectly fine and that another road surely awaited me. We hung around some of the cute, tiny restaurants that dotted the islands and stayed overnight in one of the cheaper motels we could find, since the Keys are quite elegant and expensive. I slept on the couch. They were pure gentlemen, and very funny, always joking around and singing their beloved country songs.

Once we came back, I thanked them for their attempt to help me realize my dream, even though it had turned out to be an unachievable one. I decided that it was time to set off on a road that I had caught a glimpse of when I was back in Greece years before, camping in the forest. I asked my cousin if she would take me to Miami, where Club Med's head office was located. I would try my luck at getting an interview. I didn't call ahead of time; I was resolute to let life take its course. She agreed, but was curious as to how I was going to achieve to get seen.

I strode into the square, four-story building on Blue Lagoon Drive, projecting as much determination and positive energy as I could.

"Hi, my name is C.C.," I said to the receptionist with a smile. "I'm visiting my cousin in West Palm Beach, and I decided to try my luck and see if there were any openings with Club Med at this time? I don't have an appointment, but since I was in the neighborhood I thought that I would let fate guide me. I have a degree as a tour guide, and I speak Spanish."

"Okay, just one moment," she replied with an answering smile. She spoke to another person who was in one of the adjacent offices, and then came back and sat down.

"Someone will be with you shortly," she said kindly.

I waited, chitchatting with the sympathetic receptionist until a lady came toward me.

"Hi! So you decided to come in here expecting a job just like that?" she said to me, but she was grinning.

"Actually, yes, in a way," I replied. "I was in the neighborhood, and I wanted to make sure that you meet me so that you can put a face to my resume, which you will receive soon—that is, if you don't take me now," I said, still trying to emanate as much confidence as possible without seeming overbearing.

"Wow, you are quite adventurous in your thinking," she told me, her smile getting wider. "You said that you speak Spanish? Okay then, talk to her," she said, pointing at the receptionist.

Not missing a beat, I started blabbering about where I'd learned Spanish and my adventures in Mexico with the Hispanic receptionist, and she engaged in the conversation with interest.

"Okay, okay, I see that you do speak the language very well. I think that I have something for you, but you would have to leave immediately," the other woman said to my surprise.

"Oh, well, I can't really leave immediately, but I can within a few days." I replied. "I have to fly back to Canada first, which I can do today, and then I would need a bit of time to pack and get some supplies."

"Okay, call me when you get to Canada. I will arrange for your ticket. I will send you an email as well for the clothes you will need for our themed evenings," the woman said, shaking my hand. "I am quite happy you arrived at our doorstep today, my dear. You are quite a lucky young lady."

"I will definitely be ready, and yes, I feel very lucky right now. I am so excited for this opportunity—if only you knew how long I've dreamed about this moment! Thank you so much for taking the time from your busy schedule to meet with me, I appreciate it so much," I told her while shaking her hand back with enthusiasm, nearly keeling over from excitement. I couldn't believe that I'd done it!

"No problem, and thank you, C.C. I think that you will fit in perfectly."

I thanked the receptionist profusely, as she could have sent me off as fast as I had arrived if she'd wanted to. But that is not what Club Med is all about. With a final goodbye to both women, I left the building and made my way back to my cousin's car, making sure to put on a frown before getting in; I felt like having a little fun with her.

"It's a no-go. They told me that I have to send a resume by email," I said to her while trying to keep my poker face on.

"See, I told you," she scolded. "You should have called them at least!"

"Hah! Are you kidding me? They loved me, and I'm leaving in two days! I still don't know where, though, so we need to pack up my stuff and I have to fly back ASAP. Like today!" I told her while laughing my head off. A happy, surprised grin surfaced on her beautiful face.

"*What?* Are you serious? Oh my God, I felt so bad for you! Wow. How lucky are *you?*" she said with amusement while messing up my hair.

I emailed Gigi the great news when we got home— we had broken up again by now, but we still remained friends. I flew back that evening to Montreal, where he was waiting to pick me up. As the woman at the Club Med headquarters had promised, my ticket information was in my email as well as the long list of specifics to bring with me. They were sending me to Punta Cana in Dominican Republic as a tour guide. I had less than 48 hours to get ready.

We both went shopping for my supplies the next day, since his experiences with Club Med were plentiful—he worked for the organization for many years as a diving instructor as well as an entertainer. I had to buy white, black, and red shirts as well as pants to match for themed days; silly headpieces for crazy hair days; nice clothes for Christmas and New Year's Eve; many pairs of shorts and t-shirts; bug spray and personal-care products; and all the other little things someone would need for six months. His advice was invaluable.

Club Med, spring 2001

I flew to Punta Cana in May of 2001 with butter-
flies in my stomach.

Gigi had warned me about the "troublesome
threes," which create confusion and chaos and disrupt
your end goal.

"Remember the threes, C.C.," he said to me before I
left, hugging me tightly. "After three days you will want
to leave, but it will pass. After three weeks you will again
want to leave, and again it will pass. After three months
you will have had enough and will want to quit! Stick to
it, and remember that most people feel this way. You cannot let those feelings lead you to quit. Capishe?" I think
he was envious in a way as well as happy for me, since he
knew exactly where I was going and what wonderful experiences awaited me.

Club Med played a crucial role in my life in the sense
that it smoothly transitioned me into both a place of

stillness and a place of adventure—a good mix of my life's two extremes over the past few years. It was my first job where I stayed for a whole year. In a way, I was forced to ground myself, but this time I was grounded in paradise. This is not to say that I left adventure behind; I experienced some of the craziest moments of my life during my time in Punta Cana, and, as always, I said yes to it all.

I was hypnotized by my new environment right away, starting with the Punta Cana airport, which was designed to resemble a huge, open palapa and was surrounded by palm trees swaying in the breeze. I was so happy to be there. It had been nearly ten years since my last experience with Club Med, and it felt a bit like coming home. Destiny was slowly taking its course yet again.

A bus was waiting for me and my fellow travelers who were also on their way to the Club. Upon arrival, we were greeted by the chief of the village, Hammer, who was a cool and kind-looking Canadian man. Once we reached the Club, we walked through a shielded palapa and down a long entrance corridor where I would spend every Sunday awaiting new GM's (Gentile Member). The prestigious premises looked nothing like the one I had visited in Greece ten years ago. This was a Club Med with a completely different vibe to it. Many colorful buildings of peach and white made it feel like a hotel at first. I would see soon enough why Club Med had such an esteemed reputation.

Ricardo, my manager, a Mexican guy who was much younger than I, greeted me at the end of the long, open corridor. He welcomed me to my new team and hugged me while thanking for being there. He was relieved that he had a person who spoke Spanish on his team. He showed me my new office, which was splendid; all open with two giant, solid wooden tables. This room became my home for the next year.

Next, I was shown to my room behind the main premises where all of the GO's lived. Each building housed separate rooms, shared showers, and a shared living space. My room was much more than what I had ever expected it to be—it was a really cute little loft studio. Underneath the sleeping loft was a washbasin with a medicine cabinet as well as my own toilet. I was in heaven.

I was unpacking the loads of clothes from my two hockey bags when my new next-door neighbor arrived. Her name was Sara, and she worked at the mini club with the kids. Heavyset, kind, and shy but extremely funny, she made you want to hug her right away. We really hit it off and became great friends from then on.

Once I was settled in, I decided to make my first day at Club Med a day to remember. Ricardo had told me to take the day for myself and to experience some of the Club's activities. The first thing I did was go to the beach. I explored my new home, and I felt like I belonged there already. As I passed through the halls and walkways of the Club, everyone saluted me and made me feel more than welcome. I spoke to random GO's I ran into, presenting myself as the new tour guide, which immediately endeared me to them since I was the one who would choose a couple of people to take with me on my tour excursions every week.

The beach was long and beautiful, with smooth, white sand underfoot. A little further down the beach, majestic, bushy palm trees stood next to two additional palapa structures that housed a bar and a restaurant. The first thing that struck me when I reached the beach was the ghostly shipwreck a few hundred meters from the shore. I never found out why it was there; perhaps a hurricane had beached it in the shallows.

The warm, salty, turquoise water felt amazing on my body. I was in pure ecstasy. I eventually left the beach and walked toward an intimidating trapeze structure back at the Club, where I would conquer my fear of heights. I nervously climbed the nearly forty-foot-high structure—thankfully attached at the waist by a harness—and plunged myself into the air while holding fast to the bar. I swooped down in a big arc, and the combination of being suspended so high up and the adrenalin pumping in my veins made me literally scream from joy. When I touched down into the safety net below, I was vibrating from the thrill of it. Even though I didn't get the chance to do it again, as my days were soon to be filled with numerous activities that kept me busy, I'll never forget that feeling.

I went to get something to eat in one of the restaurants, and the food was exquisite. French chefs prepared a variety of excellent, mouthwatering cuisine, which they meticulously presented on the tables. Us GO's had the chance to savor delicious French wines, as well—as long as we didn't overindulge. One of our duties included sitting with GM's for meals, and no one ever questioned us having a glass of rosé with the guests.

Club Med prides itself in being different and unique, and one of the ways the organization accomplishes this is by treating the GM's—or gentile members—like family, which creates a sense of belonging. All of the GO's were always on their toes making the guests feel at home every minute of the day. We even had the village clown, Cali, a hilarious, thin-as-a-toothpick French youngster who had a gift for coming up with unique ways to entertain each and every guest.

We ate with them, we listened to them, we told them all about other Clubs from around the world, we danced with them, laughed with them, and even cried with and comforted them when the rare emergency on the premises like 9/11, would temporarily shift the whole world into madness. We still found ways to balance those heartbreaking moments with reengaging the guests in the joys of their surroundings. It was this type of mentality and devotion that appealed to the guests and created such an appealing atmosphere and experience.

Unlike my experience at the all-inclusive resort where I had worked in Mexico just a short time before Punta Cana, our involvement with and total dedication to our guests here was entirely distinct. Even though my official title was Tour Guide, my duties went far beyond this, and I began to understand what Gigi had warned me about. Because of our extreme devotion and attentiveness to every single detail, it soon became a heavy weight to bear. We as human beings inevitably have good and bad days, but here, there was no such thing as having a bad day. We were, however, given the occasional day off for unavoidable problems, such as particularly bad PMS for the female staff. Since I was susceptible to severe symptoms due to a hormonal imbalance I believe I inherited from my grandmother, let's just say that I didn't receive many compliments on my utmost devotion to customer service on those weeks.

When I wasn't on my tours, I was handing out plates of succulent fresh fruit around the Club for the guests sitting on their long chairs by the beach or by the enormous pool with its little wooden bridge. I constantly tried to involve every person from the Club in our activities; not one person was left behind or unattended. I usually chose the beach to do my good deeds, since I loved the water so much. I would randomly grab a GM by the hand and take them out on the small sailing boats for a little ride, where we would often observe rays gently zooming through the water below us.

When I wasn't on the beach or handing out plates of nibbles or conversing with GM's, I was practicing my dances for the evening shows with the rest of the crew. We practiced tirelessly in order to produce somewhat quality entertainment for our beloved GM's. Every day we devised something new. My first show was "Gone with the Wind" with a comedic spin. Our talented and jovial seamstress Sandra, a young dark haired girl with turquoise eyes, took pride in the creation of our gorgeous costumes and even let them out when we needed a little extra room—the delicious food, especially the famous, scrumptious white chocolate bread in the mornings, made us pack on a few extra pounds.

We would often invite the funnier guests as well the more reserved ones to be part of the show that evening or the next, dressing them up and guiding them through the process. Many of these people would become our friends for life, sending us letters letting us know how they were doing in their lives as well as sometimes inviting us to their homes.

Some shows we put on were more for adults, like the one with the gynecologist giving driving directions to his friend while examining a patient—which was hilarious. Others were set on the beach with water bottles as our fountains and tunics for our costumes, just like Greek gods and goddesses. Another was a fashion show, which was one of my favorites, and we also had our own version of the Golden Globes with funny sketches and projections.

One time we had an event where the girls stayed to entertain the Club while the guys had a night out. Boy, did we do a number with the GM's—it was a sexy pajama-themed party where we came up with a host of original activities, up to and including body shots. I won't go into details, but it was a really fun night. Nothing dirty, but we all ventured a little bit outside of our comfort zones and created a night to remember for everyone.

Each show ended with the Club Med song, "Haut les Mains," as well as a couple of others, and right after the show at around ten o'clock we would all make our way to the bar and disco where we had other activities for the GM's prepared, which sometimes lasted until the early hours of the morning.

We were given a pack of tickets every so often that were redeemable at the bar, and with these we could have a drink or two with our GM's. I quickly made friends with Mauricio, the bartender—a man with whom I formed a casual relationship. A lot of the GO's found themselves partners for the season, and many of these partnerships developed into long-term relationships and marriages. This was not the case for me. I was there to have fun, and sure enough, I found the right people for that purpose. This is where my "Mata Hari" skills truly developed—I wasn't going to become someone else's toy. They were going to become mine.

The only time I ever got out of my bar duties was when I had an early morning the next day for one of my tours to Santo Domingo, the capital. Besides the chefs, I was the only one who had to wake up that early. I made sure that I had all of my people with me and that they had all had something to eat before leaving for the two-hour bus ride. During the trip, I would point out the country's flora and fauna and tell them as much as possible about the surrounding area, sometimes juggling between three different languages. Even though most of our patrons were from France and the United States, we did get the odd few from Italy, Spain, Argentina, and Mexico. Because I was the only one who spoke Spanish at the time in my team, I became responsible for most of the Spanish-speaking guests' tours.

In the beginning, I was uneasy with my general lack of knowledge; however, I familiarized myself by tagging along on my coworkers' tours, and soon I became comfortable with my new job. In this, I saw a window of opportunity in which my past could help me to create a new and original version of me. Very quickly I realized I had something exclusive to offer my beloved guests on top of my coveted Spanish skills. My pure sense of adventure as well as the yearning for danger and excitement that was always brewing in my veins led me to try things others absolutely refused to do.

Santo Domingo wasn't my favorite excursion. Although a beautiful colonial city with a rich history, it was still a city, and I loved to be in the jungle most of all. Nevertheless, it definitely had its interesting elements. The city was founded by Bartholomew Columbus, Christopher Columbus's brother, who has a bronze statue dedicated to him in the city's main square. Santo Domingo is one of the oldest cities in the Caribbean. The Colonial Zone, declared a World Heritage Site by UNESCO, is at the heart of the city. Beautiful structures from the 1500s humble you at every turn, including the first cathedral built in the New World. It was called Ciudad Trujillo during Trujillo's dictatorship from 1936 to 1961, but after his assassination the city reclaimed its old name.

The city's Colonial Zone has a very old vibe to it while still feeling vibrant and interesting—the upbeat atmosphere, with sounds of cheerful Bachata and merengue music always hovering in the air, makes it a very pleasant place to spend time.

When we could come to the city, our beloved Chantal—a petite, feisty French woman who had decided to stay in Santo Domingo when she met and fell in love with a Dominican man—would be waiting for us at the cathedral. From there, she would lead us throughout the beautiful city, as she was the city's official tour guide. She had a gorgeous blue-eyed son who took over her duties whenever she was busy. She would affectionately call him "chocolate" because of his light-brown, chocolaty skin. Chantal opened her house to wandering and homeless kids who came to her for help as well as for her motherly advice and affection. I think that she still has a co-op there for kids, and is significantly involved in the city's programs for the young.

One of my more casual tours was the catamaran excursion, where we drank, danced, sang, and swam in the gorgeous waters of the Caribbean. It was a shorter drive out to where we would launch the huge catamaran, and we would meet up with our private entertainer there. She was a young, spirited Dominican girl who, when she moved her hips to the rhythm of the energetic Bachata, seemed to be missing a few bones in her lower body. Her graceful, fluid movements made what was probably incredibly skilled work look effortless. When we tried to emulate her, most of us looked like two-by-fours on the dance floor. Thank God that she took the time to teach me a few moves! Because of this, my love for that type of dance emerged; I still love it to this day. We would come back to the Club completely drunk on the delicious local rum, which we'd been sipping on since ten o'clock in the morning. My responsibility of making sure that none of the guests got too tipsy failed royally, since I wasn't very good at that myself.

The tour that became my favorite was to Quisqueya in the province of San Pedro de Macoris. This excursion took us out into the jungle, where I made friends with the host, a thin, older French man by the name of Christophe. I spent some of my most memorable moments of the year in this area. On my days off, which I looked forward to every week, I would rent a car the day before and then right after my dance and bar duties were fulfilled I would drive to the jungle and spend a whole night and day in my own little slice of paradise.

The tour consisted of around an hour drive to the tiny, underprivileged village of El Gato, with its forty inhabitants who lived in truly meager homes that they had constructed with whatever they could find—a puzzle of wood, metal, and bricks. The tiny school, which was the size of a standard bedroom in a Western house, was made of cement and had only a few tables inside for the children. There was no library and few supplies, but the kids still had huge smiles on their faces and always greeted us with curiosity.

Libio, one of the villagers who worked for Christophe, had the responsibility of greeting us as well as guiding us through his one-road village. He always had his mascot, a rooster, with him. He had a new one with him nearly every week, since cockfighting was legal and wildly popular throughout the country. People took care of those roosters better than they took care of themselves and took immense pride in them. Long metal spurs were attached to the roosters' feet, making the sport even bloodier. The animal lover inside of me struggled with this, and it was difficult to keep my opinions on the subject hidden. I had to accept that cockfighting was part of their way of life, however, and somewhat embrace the Dominicans' love for the sport.

On one of our tours, Libio brought us to the end of the steep, curvy dirt road, where a little boat that looked like a smaller version of a pontoon craft with a roof welcomed us onto the green river, which was surrounded by a thick forest. We let the gentle current transport us, making a stop at a huge, tilted tree that was practically made for a rope swing. We climbed a couple of feet up into it, and Libio passed us the rope. Laughing, we swung out over the water and plunged ourselves into the refreshing depths. It was quite a popular spot. After that, we continued drifting toward our final destination: Christophe's house, which was right on the edge of the river.

His two-story wooden home was quite rustic, with chickens running around and his pet crow in the downstairs area, who would constantly caw at anyone who dared to get close to him. There were horses, as well, and we would ride them around the vast property. He also had kayaks, which the GM's used to paddle around the river. Christophe made sure we had enough to eat, as well, cooking up delicious freshwater shrimp from the river in the Cajun style that no one could ever get enough of.

Following the tug of my curious streak, I soon learned from the locals about the various creatures that lived inside the ground all around us. Armed with a bottle of water and a cup, I went looking for them, the locals having taught me how to catch what I was looking for. I searched until I found a distinctive hole, and then I slowly started to pour water inside the cavity. And there it was: a not-so-happy brown tarantula emerging from her home, disturbed by the water. She slowly crawled onto my outstretched palm, and I gently picked her up. Her body was the size of my whole hand, and she stayed on it while I proudly presented her to the audience that surrounded me until I set her free again a few minutes later.

My second creature was a very weird-looking one: a vinegar scorpion. By its name, you can imagine the odor it produces when it feels threatened. I wouldn't pick this guy up with my bare hands—that's what the cup was for. I always found one to show my GM's whenever I went searching. You could find them hiding in the decaying trees and other vegetation on the ground. The vinegar scorpions are small, flat creatures with long legs and, unlike their more common cousins, they have thin tails at the end of their wide bodies and smaller claws.

The one creature that even the locals thought I was *loca* for pursuing was the creepy, long, orange-and-red millipede. I must have had a death wish where pushing the limits of my adventures was concerned, because the millipedes were the most dangerous living things in the area. The critters even chased after the poor chickens.

Since I was known as the one who always took the crazy risks, GM's would arrive at the Club having heard the legend of the tour guide who chases tarantulas, vinegar scorpions, and millipedes and would make sure to reserve the day I was touring Quisqueya.

There were always new and exciting things just around the corner. On one of my days off with Christophe and Libio, my adventurous spirit led me to participate in one of the most unique things I've ever witnessed: a gaga. A gaga is a type of musical festival hailing from Haiti, the name of which means "not in the right mind." When you partake in this activity, the combination of the rum, the different types of homemade musical instruments like bamboo and metal trumpets, maracas, drums, and metal bells, and the spirited dances put you in a sort of trance. These gagas usually took place in the middle of the large sugarcane fields all over the country. It was quite an exciting event to be a part of.

— ~

Even the exciting and joyous nature of my surroundings during my time with Club Med in the Dominican

Republic couldn't save me from the restlessness that soon plagued me, just as Gigi had predicted it would. I was unable to ride them out as he had advised, however, because once again, my past was rearing its ugly head in the form of making me feel like I had to run away again. My flashbacks had returned, and they were draining me both emotionally and physically. I tried to mask these troubling feelings with sex, which inevitably only further contributed to a joyless mindset.

I'd had enough. It was time to roll up my sleeves and do something about it. I decided that I wasn't returning to the Club—instead, I would travel to Europe. I didn't know what awaited me there; all I knew was that something was calling me, and I was going to find out what it was.

I left the Club in May of 2002, more confused than ever, feeling as if I was drifting out at sea once again. I called my mother, packed up a little backpack, and followed the sound of that indistinct but compelling call.

June, 2002

With Gigi's beautiful farewell words still in my ears from our call, I settled in to pass the three hours that remained before my flight with a renewed sense of confidence in my decision. I gazed out at the planes through the large window, pondering the next three months and my 30th birthday. It didn't take long for my old friend confusion to make itself known. I really needed to find my way, but how? Why was it so difficult for me? Why couldn't I just make peace with my past once and for all and then move on?

We finally boarded, and as the plane took off, so did my tears. During the long flight, I couldn't help but feel like a bottle that was about to be uncorked—a bottle with a message of freedom inside that had been thrown to the tides of the universe. With Enya singing softly to me in my headphones, I emptied out tear after tear from my aching soul, hiding from the rest of the passengers under a blanket.

One of the movies shown on the flight was *The Time Machine*, which is about a man who tries to change his past by returning to it until he realizes that he can do nothing to change what has already happened. He did, however, have the power to change his future. I knew that I needed to do the same, but how? How could I make peace with the monsters of my past?

I stayed under the blanket for the whole flight.

Upon arriving in Rome, I took the train from the airport to the central station to catch yet another train for Lamezia, where my friend Frank from Club Med was waiting for me. I had emailed him to see if I could visit him at the Club where he worked. On the way, I met a couple of Canadian girls travelling to Africa to meet up with their boyfriends. Once again, I was temporarily transported by dreams of new and exciting adventures—this time in Africa—hearing about their plans. But that was not my destiny.

Finally on the train from Rome to Lamezia, I met a man named Mateo. We started talking a bit, but he was more interested in reading his newspaper. He lent me a page but I was too tired to read, and I soon fell asleep for the next three hours, oblivious to the wonderful scenery passing me by.

Mateo woke me up when my stop was coming up, and he invited me for a cappuccino in the next wagon. A few minutes later I arrived at my destination and we disembarked. Mateo realized that he had missed his train, so he invited me for more coffee. We sat down in a cute little outdoor café next to the station. There, I ate real Italian pizza for the first time while waiting for my friend to pick me up. I chatted with Mateo, took in my beautiful surroundings—I felt great at the time, as Italians are very friendly people, and the men...well, let's just say that Mateo wasn't hard on the eyes.

Eventually I saw my friend pull up in his beautiful red Jaguar, and after a few somewhat formal introductions, Frank sat with us while sipping on a cappuccino. Before I left, Mateo handed me a piece of paper with his phone number on it and invited me to spend a few days with him in Rome. I thanked him, and Frank and I left for the Club. I never saw Mateo again.

Upon arriving at the Club, I immediately felt extremely out of place. Every cell in my body was screaming at me to leave, and to leave fast. It was quite an alarming feeling—I only know that something inside of me knew that this was not the place I was supposed to be.

A few days later, Frank dropped me off at the same train station.

I stared up into the sky, having no idea of what to do or where to go next.

I had no plan B. I could have gone to Africa if I'd wanted to, but a little voice inside my head—or perhaps my heart—suggested Greece. I listened to it and decided to head back to the land of the gods once more.

First, I had to get to the Italian port city of Bari—a place that will forever be engraved on my heart as the location of one of my most meaningful moments at the beginning of my healing process. I called my sister, letting her know that I would soon be arriving and that I would call her again once I had established what my next move was.

It was June 12th, 2002.

The trip to Bari took about five hours. During this time I stayed next to the open window in the hall of the train, where the smell of oil turned your stomach. I became hypnotized by the squeaky sounds of the machinery as well as by the spectacular landscapes of Italy's east coast. I remember nothing specific about the trip, however, because my mind was lost in dark daydreams, unable to fully process reality.

I arrived in Bari and somehow found my way to the port, still in my zombielike state of mind. I felt lost in every sense of the word. I just didn't care anymore.

I was headed straight for disaster.

I walked through the small town, dodging travellers in search of their own adventures, and located the ferry terminal. I bought myself a ticket, which included a cabin so that I could rest for the fifteen hours of sailing. I boarded the boat and went straight to my cabin; I was exhausted and deeply depressed. I wanted to crawl into a hole and die. I decided that I would just stay in my cabin for the whole trip and cry my pathetic tears. But the reality of the situation was different: I needed to figure out a way to get from Patras to Pireas, which was a distance of about 207 kilometers, and I had no idea how I was going to manage this in order to meet up with my sister.

I had to find a lift soon, but I still told myself that I would be fine. *Once I arrive, there will be someone with whom I can hitch a ride*, I told myself as I settled into my cabin. After taking a much-needed shower to wash off the dust from the long train ride, I just wanted to lay down my head. But the restless little voice in my head kept hollering at me to get up and go outside—I didn't know why. Too tired to argue with my own demons, I listened to the voice and left my cabin.

It was five minutes to eight in the evening when I went out onto the deck; there was a pack of stray dogs playing on the dock, greeting the passengers with wiggly tails and lolling tongues in farewell. I imagine there were people around me, but I ignored them; I wanted to be alone with my thoughts, and I couldn't care less if the world fell on my head in that moment. I knew that I needed to do some smooth talking to find a ride from one of the other passengers, but I was so tired of being polite, nice, and proper. *I will walk if I have to*, I thought to myself preposterously.

I watched the sunset behind Bari's port on the horizon, clutching the rails with my hands until my knuckles turned white. My heart was aching, my soul was tired, and my mind was still searching for—and not finding—the answers I sought. Who am I, why did all those terrible things happen to me, why do I have this constant hunger to leave the beautiful places I wind up when there is no one, nothing, and nowhere to go back to...What is my destiny, and how do I face it?

I must have been on the deck for over an hour, lost in my thoughts among the presence of ghosts. I was in my own world—a hazy, dark place, so empty of love, empty of lasting friendship, empty of happiness...just empty.

As I stared at the hypnotizing movement of the water, I felt myself leaning forward. I wondered how it would feel to just resign from life, to take all of that confusion and self-loathing and give it to the Mediterranean, thus relieving the agonizing pain in my chest.

But no. Although the thought of suicide had crossed my mind from time to time in my life, it never really went beyond that—a thought. I knew that, in taking my own life, I would be punishing myself for other peoples' misdeeds and hurting the ones I cared for in the process. In that moment, looking over the railing at the churning waves below, I decided I would not condemn myself with this selfish act.

A Cry for Help

*P*lease, God...please help me, help me, I beg of you! Please help me to make and find peace in my life...please! I screamed at the top of my lungs inside my head.

Ask and you shall receive, they say.

The universe was listening—it responded by sending me an angel. He seemed to fall straight from the sky at the exact moment when I needed help the most. Obviously, he wasn't really an angel, nor did he literally fall out of the sky, but it certainly felt like it.

The man must have been standing next to me the whole time; I was just oblivious to his existence up until that moment. In the same second I was thinking *help!* up into the sky with all the strength I had left, a cup of beer from the table next to me spilled on my leg..I looked up, and there he was, a very handsome young man in his late twenties or early thirties looking down at me with the most beautiful, piercing blue eyes I'd ever seen. He had a tall, slim build with a slight hunch to his shoulders, strong facial features, and a concerned tilt to his tight lips.

I'm not sure how the cup of beer got knocked over— the strange part was that there was absolutely no wind or turbulence from the ferry. I guess God was with me on that ferry and heard my cries that day.

With an extremely strong German accent, the man said, "Oh, I am sorry," indicating the spilled beer.

"It's okay," I replied, wiping myself dry. "You are German, yes?" I asked, groping around for something to say.

"Yes, I am," he said, his voice serious but kind.

"Hum, where are you going?" I continued, not wanting to miss any chance of securing a lift. Somehow I already felt good about this man, with his angelic eyes that looked strangely familiar. I trusted him right away.

"I am going to Athens," he said. Wow, was that music to my ears. I decided to pursue the chance of hitching a ride with him. Maybe I would feel better once I'd reached Athens and had been reunited with my sister.

"Oh yes? I am also going to Athens. How are you getting there?"

"Vit my kar," he said in his strong accent.

"Well, I am actually looking for someone to take me to Athens, as I haven't secured a ride yet." I hoped that he wouldn't mind me being so forward.

He nodded and said in a kind tone, "I can take you vit me if you vant, but only until Athens because I need to get to the port, I am taking a ship to Santorini."

"That would be great," I said, relieved. "I will take the bus from there, I am sure it is not very expensive. Do you have a cabin here?"

"No, I just have a seat," he said, a hint of caution creeping into his voice.

"If you want, you can use the second bunk bed in my cabin to rest. It would be like an exchange for the ride, and you will be rested for your trip," I said, genuinely wishing to offer him something in return for his kindness. At this moment I felt his whole being take a step backwards without him actually moving. He seemed to be examining my saneness; you could actually see his eyes saying, "Uh oh, this girl is crazy!"

"What's wrong?" I asked, noting his discomfort.

"It does not bother you," he said, "that I am a man, and you are a voman?"

"No, I don't see any problem with this," I replied truthfully. "You need sleep, and I have an extra bunk bed that is useless to me. Like I said, it would be like an exchange of favors."

"Ve vill see later," he responded, though he seemed to be considering my offer.

In all honestly, I couldn't have cared less if I got raped—it wouldn't have been a new experience for me, and I felt dead inside anyway. But somehow I still trusted this man not to hurt me nevertheless.

It was beginning to get chilly outside, so we decided to go to the terrace in the back for a beer.

"I have to go the vashroom. Can you vatch my things?" he asked. I nodded, and once he left I gathered his bag and jacket closer to mine so that no one could get to them while he was gone. It was weeks later that he told me that he never went to the washroom, but instead wanted to see what I would do with his belongings. It was then that he realized I was not crazy or trying to seduce and rob him, but just a lost soul in whom he could place his confidence.

"That is ven I realized the voman you are," he said when he told me the truth about that moment on the ferry, "because you did exactly vat I vish my vife vould do one day."

When he came back from the "vashroom," we chatted idly, and the conversation drifted toward his planned trip to Santorini.

"Have you ever been?" he asked.

"No, I never had the chance to, but I hope to go there one day," I replied, feeling a little twinkle of my old adventurous self waking up within me.

"Vell, you absolutely have to go to Santorini. It is a magnificent place that fills you up vit marvelous feelings."

"That sounds lovely. I will go one day for sure," I replied. I had always wanted to see this part of Greece that I'd only seen on postcards, and the idea of visiting brought a smile to my face.

"Vy don't you come vit me?" he asked, apparently wary of me no more.

"Wow, that's direct, isn't it?" I said, taken aback. "To answer your question, it's simple: I don't have the money for that right now."

"You don't need money except for your own personal expenses. The room is already paid for, and the ferry is not that expensive. Think about it, he continued, "it vill be good for your soul." He looked at me with sympathy but not pity, perhaps feeling how lost I was in the universe at this juncture.

"I will think about it, and we will see," I replied, brushing the subject off for now, the intensity of his blue gaze making me feel uneasy. I wasn't ready for it yet.

After some reflection on the offer, I realized that I had no reason *not* to go with my new friend. I could go back to Athens, or I could take what seemed like an excellent opportunity for me to get away from everything, truly rethink my life, and do whatever I needed to do to change. The tree of destiny had gently extended a branch to me in the form of this man, so I decided to grasp it. I felt like a bottle bouncing along on the waves of a raging ocean once more, but this time, maybe I was heading for shore instead of further out to sea. I had absolutely nothing to lose.

The uncanny confidence I had in this man's good intentions made me want to share his company. My instincts were telling me *go, go, go!* Just as they had told me to leave Italy, but this time they were screaming out loud to follow, not run. *This is where you are supposed to be, with this man, right now,* they seemed to say.

After a few hours more of casual conversation and sipping on our beers, I blurted out, "Yes! I will go with you. The only thing is, I really am not able to spend a lot of money."

He smiled as if to reassure me and said, "I am very happy you made this decision. You vill see. You vill like it, and it vill change your life as it did mine."

And that is how I ended up in Santorini a day and a half later.

An Illuminating Decision

We sat on a bench, listening to the waves caressing the ship's sides. Somehow it seemed appropriate for me to lie down and put my head on his knees. After a couple of minutes he put his hands in my hair. We stayed like that for about an hour or so until we decided it was time to go to sleep. We were tired, and we had to get some rest before the long drive the next day.

I went straight to bed when we entered the cabin and put the blanket over half of my face. Perhaps feeling my weariness, he sat beside me on the edge of the bed, caressing my hair again.

I watched him. *Who are you*, I thought to myself. The answer came as clear as if someone was speaking right next to my ear. "He is your angel, my dear—your personal German angel to help you on your path to freeing your soul."

While he contemplated me, he leaned in and softly declared, "I vant you to know that I have no desire to make love to you or to hurt you. I am not a one-night-stand man, so you can relax and sleep peacefully."

Indeed, he was not. He was absolutely nothing like the other men from my past. I felt secure, protected, and so peaceful—I truly cannot express it in words. I knew that something was about to change drastically within me, and it was a wonderful feeling. With that thought, I fell into a deep sleep.

I woke up a short time later; probably last night's beer. The light was still on. He was sleeping but looked a little cold, so I grabbed a blanket and gently covered him up. He awakened momentarily, just enough for a small glance with warmth in his eyes that said "thank you," to which I had no choice but to reply with an affectionate smile. I fell asleep for a few more hours.

We woke up nearly at the same time in the morning. He took a quick shower.

"Take your time. Ven you're ready I vill be at the same place from last night vaiting for you. Okay?" he said to me.

I nodded, and then I spent the next hour getting ready. It was only about a week later that Ralph jokingly informed me that when a man tells you to "take as much time as you need," it's usually only a figure of speech.

I gathered my stuff so that I would be ready for the arrival in Patras and walked through the labyrinth of the ship's hallways, joining him precisely where we had met the night before. I ordered myself a coffee, which is a rarity in my case—but then again, I would experience many rarities over the course of the next month. We chitchatted for a bit and fetched our belongings from the cabin. We went down the steep iron stairs to an area where numerous cars were parked. We entered his fine-looking blue Alfa Romeo station wagon, which smelled of new car. We then waited over an hour for our turn to exit the ship's belly.

I loved his car—it suited him perfectly and was distinguished, humble, beautiful, and charming, just like Ralph. When we finally disembarked we drove away from the traffic and were swiftly off onto the road toward Piraeus.

The Journey of a Lifetime

The road along the Peloponnesian peninsula from Patras to Piraeus was a delight for my eyes. I was home. Greece had played such a crucial role in my life that my overall feelings toward it couldn't be anything but fond and familiar. It will always be this way, forever engraved on my heart—and with this journey, Greece would take on an even deeper meaning still.

We didn't talk much during the drive. We stopped for a break, and I called my sister to let her know that I would not be joining her in Athens as we had discussed and that I would not be coming back for a week or so because I was going to Santorini.

"Are you sure that's what you want? Do you trust this guy?" she asked me, a bit puzzled; of course, she also knew my tendency to do crazy things.

"Yes, this is what I want, Maya. And yes, I do trust him," I reassured her.

"Well, be careful, and call me if you need anything," she implored, and then we said our goodbyes. I felt much better after the call; I was anticipating the conversation to go much worse than it had, and I didn't want to justify my decision to her.

We got back on the road accompanied by melodic Greek songs from Haris Alexiou, Despina Vandi, Laura Pausini's "Volvere Junto A Ti", as well as by his favorite, Klaus Hoffmann's "Komm wir reiten den Wind" (Come, let's ride the wind), which would soon enough become mine as well. I was swept away by the stunning view of the different hues of blue of the Mediterranean Sea, the majesty of the semi-treeless rocky cliffs, and the familiar aromas entering the car of jasmine, lavender, and thyme—everything blending together to welcome us back to the land of the gods.

We made our way through noisy, polluted Piraeus along with the many other trucks and cars trying to reach their ships just like us. Enduring the hustle and bustle, we finally purchased our tickets and then sat down on the outside terrace in one of the main taverns on the premises. I ordered a beer; I am not usually a beer drinker, but this one was very refreshing after the long road trip. I needed to write to my best friend Cécile, who was in Montreal, and tell her about my newest adventure.

Cécile had a slim build with larger hips, was quite tall, and was a bit "witchy" looking, with her deep-brown eyes and wavy auburn hair. She'd arrived in Canada from France full of hope for new opportunities in a new country—hopes that unfortunately hadn't panned out as well as she would have liked, as she'd been met with nothing but struggle since she'd relocated.

We met in college while I was getting my tour-guide certificate and quickly became good friends. Everyone, including myself, thought she was from another planet, with her intense originality and funny bohemian look. She loved her solitude, and was a bit of a lost soul like me, never seeming to grasp the next rung on the ladder, always struggling with one thing or another. She was my best friend—still is—and we supported each other in all our endeavors.

I realized that I had to tell her all about this wonderful new predicament I had put myself in and let her know that I was all right. Luckily, inside the café was an Internet station. Unluckily, it proved to be from the age of the dinosaurs; I think most turtles go faster than that connection did.

Our departure was at 7:00 p.m., so we opted for another beer before heading out to our ferry. Boarding the ferry with a car felt just like trying to shove hundreds of beans through a tiny funnel. We followed each other closely: cars, trucks, bikes, motorcycles, and people all desperately trying to find a way inside the ferry, which looked more like a dungeon than a boat. We finally parked the car and went out onto the higher deck to observe the commotion below us. I was feeling lighthearted and extremely delighted to have this opportunity for another new adventure. At this point, however, I was still oblivious to the fact that this adventure—unlike all of my previous ones—was for my soul to experience a painful yet vital transformation.

We left with the view of the Grecian coastline behind us, its white cement houses getting smaller and smaller. I had the privilege to witness the seagulls waltzing in the sunset behind the ship, almost within reach. They frantically dove into the agitated sea to get at the fish that had surfaced from the ferry's engines. I watched each of the serene performers fall further and further behind as we got further and further from the port.

We sat down in the open area on the higher deck of the ferry. Beside me was a couple holding a bag of delicious-looking cherries, for which I offered a few euros. It had been a long time since I'd tasted the exquisite, juicy red fruit. They were delicious.

We stayed out on the deck, and the suffocating heat from earlier was very quickly replaced by the cold of the night, even in the Mediterranean summer. I lay down on Ralph's legs and he covered me with his blanket as well as my huge red towel that my mom had given me, and I fell into a deep sleep. He kept my thick, wavy hair in his hand so that the wind wouldn't toss it around and wake me up.

I was startled awake some time later by booming, thumping noises coming from close by. The noise was coming from a DJ out on the deck who decided to promote Ios, a "party island", for all the youngsters who want to dance all night and not give a damn about tomorrow. The DJ's sound system was impressively loud, and—well, I wasn't exactly in the mood for dance music. But for those who wanted to dance, it was perfect. Almost everyone on the boat started to move to the echoing rhythm.

We observed four young passengers in front of us; one was a handsome boy and one not so much, and their female companions mirrored them in this. We started to analyze their behavior—the strategies, the little jealousies, the seductions, the reactions to and from one another—and we soon enough understood their love games.

After a while I needed to stretch my legs, so I walked to the end of the deck; you know, the same place where Rose climbed up and leaned over the edge in *Titanic*. I, on the other hand, did not climb over the railing, nor did I have the desire to jump this time. Ralph came to join me, and it was at this point that my "therapy sessions" with him started.

He asked me the same questions as many others have done throughout my life, but somehow this time, I reacted very differently, and tears started to run down my cheeks as soon as I started talking. These were not the last tears he drew from me. I didn't know where to start; there was so much to be revealed. I ended up beginning my story with this:

"I saw things and experienced events in my life at a young age that a little girl should not have to. I don't want to talk about them now, though, okay?" I felt somewhat defensive.

"Okay," he said kindly, understanding and respecting my boundaries.

All of a sudden, a flow of ghastly memories came flooding through me. It felt like hell—my stories, my history, my life. The life and the heart of that little girl from Slovakia was still inside me, and she was broken; she needed healing.

I had only ever told my story to people in vague terms while working at Club Med the previous year. But this time was different—this journey, which I felt had been calling to me from far away for so long, was to once and for all mend the little girl with the confused, broken soul. It was finally time to open the Pandora's box of my past and to release the demons within in order to send that little girl off into the world as a brand new person— as a woman.

This transformation was not going to happen in an instant, however. Ralph just looked at me for a while as I continued to stare out at the vast, dark sea behind the ferry, still struggling with how to put words to the enormity of what I had to face.

Majestic Santorini Awaits

We finally arrived in Santorini. He gently grasped my hand and squeezed it, like he was silently telling me to "hang on to your horses, this island will completely shift your soul." It was four in the morning. The island seemed peculiar at first; not like any other in the Cyclades. The largest volcanic eruption of the sixteenth century formed this island into what was to become our home for the next five weeks. The bottom of the island was almost completely uninhabited except for the tiny port housing a restaurant and a couple of houses; the rest of the area was a sharp, glorious, rocky cliff.

The tip of the island seemed like it was covered by snow at first glance, but once you looked closer, you could clearly see that the "snow" was actually a scattering of typical Greek houses in blends of whites and splashes of blue covering this magnificent place.

The mix of excitement and unease that had kept me company since we'd boarded the ferry persisted. We got into his car, disembarked from the belly of the dragon—a little better organized this time since there was not much space to maneuver the cars around each other—and parked the car to the left of the pier. We walked to one of the few café restaurants that his Albanian friend owned, who joined us about an hour later.

We stayed there for a time, sipping on coffee and watching the ferry empty out. We would be spending many more days at this café, doing the same thing as we were now. An awe-inspiring feeling was creeping up on me, like I somehow knew that my time spent on this island with Ralph would be a monumental stepping-stone for the next chapter of my life.

We left at around 9:00 a.m., driving along an extremely steep, zigzagged hill. It reminded me of Lombard Street in San Francisco, but higher and longer. Music playing and windows rolled down, we made our way from the pier upward toward the beautiful white houses we'd identified earlier, heading in the direction of Kamari. Ralph visited "the mother of my heart," as he called Santorini, a few times each year. This was his twelfth visit to the island in five years.

At this point, I was exhausted and just wanted a bed to sleep in. We arrived in Kamari, a beautiful little tourist village along the coast with a mysterious feel to it. The beach was covered with black and red lava pebbles, and numerous taverns were nestled along the main road for the many tourists to stop into, rest, and have a cooling drink.

We went to meet up with Sofia, the woman he had rented from every time he had set foot on the island. Ralph's space was a little studio on the street behind the beach, next to the restaurant Splash Bar, where we would spend the next five weeks eating our breakfasts. The studio was very cute; we had an ocean view, a little kitchenette that we seldom used, two beds, and a balcony where we spent our evenings playing tavli, a game similar to backgammon.

Upon arriving, I had a second wind, and we decided to rent a moped and go for a ride. Santorini is truly a unique and magical place, with its snowy white houses perched on top of the long-dead volcano and the magnificent Mediterranean sea, which, from the top of the island, looks like millions of sparkling blue stars shining back at you for you to admire.

Fira, the capital, is much more commercial than Oia, which has a more laid-back, artistic feel to it. People from all over the world have made it their home, and many say that they live like "poor kings." The inhabitants of Oia have established businesses to suit their clientele like little cafés, ateliers, galleries, and all sorts of stores. It really does have that bohemian feel to it, and I enjoyed spending a day there. Oia also had the most beautiful sunsets I've ever seen; because of its location at the end of the island, the sun sets smoothly into the sea and slowly paints a mood before your eyes, almost like a symphony that only your soul can hear. It is absolutely breathtaking.

That same evening, we came back to our sanctuary in Kamari and went for supper in one of the many restaurants hidden from the hustle and bustle on the main avenue—a cute little place where our outside table on the terrace was already waiting for us. We had the Santorini special, "Santorini Balls," which are delicious fried tomato patties. We ordered a bottle of wine and some ouzo—a refreshing Greek anisette liquor—to which you need to add water. Since I hadn't yet slept much on top of the general intensity of my new surroundings, the alcohol went straight to my head, I must admit.

Our first official outing was quite charming. We finished our supper around midnight and happily walked toward our studio through the animated evening activities taking place in the village. As Ralph opened the door to the studio, I went in for a (slightly sloppy) kiss. In my inebriated state of mind, I thought that no man in this world would bring a girl with him on a trip like this without expecting anything from her at some point. I didn't even have time to try for another, however, because before I knew it, he was tenderly pushing me away.

"It is not because I don't vant or desire you," Ralph said softly, "and it is not because you are not beautiful. I just vant you to know that, at this time, I cannot make love to you. Know that you can have peace here, and find your vay." I felt like I must have reeked from a combination of desperation, loneliness, confusion, and, of course, alcohol for him to push me away like this; rejection was an entirely a new concept for me to grasp, and to tell you the truth, it kind of bruised my ego.

This was the last time we ever came close to an embrace. Instead, the gradual progression of a flourishing sexless relationship was born throughout the next five weeks in each other's company. It was a relationship completely fulfilled outside of physical pleasure. There was a genuine tenderness between us that we shared with our eyes and through just being together. To my surprise and delight, I discovered mental, emotional, and spiritual love for the first time—a once-in-a-lifetime experience.

I perceived a hint of sadness in his eyes that night—a sadness that I came to only scratch the surface of later on, as he never let me in deeper. He encouraged me to open up to him completely, however, and I couldn't help but accept his invitation. I called him my German angel, and he would one day call me his Canadian Sunshine.

This is our story.

The Beginning

The next morning when I got up, Ralph was already ready to leave for Splash Bar next door.

"Take your time," he said with a cheeky little smile that said *...but not all your time.* "I vill be waiting for you at this table right there," he continued while showing me the table from the balcony.

I showered, put on my green sundress from the Dominican Republic, which I wore pretty much the whole time I was in Santorini, and went to join him. It was very warm and extremely bright out. I sat down at our table while he continued reading his German newspaper with only a glance as a welcome. I saw a plate of breakfast in front of him, but I was not hungry so I had a smoke instead.

"You must eat. Breakfast is the most important meal. It vill give you energy for the day, and energy for your mind. Yes?" he said to me in his slightly stumbling English when he looked up from his newspaper. I had to work hard to fully distinguish his words in the beginning, but somehow I came to understand him more when he was silent.

"Yes, I know, but I will eat in a couple of minutes," I said. He nodded and continued reading his newspaper. I stared out at the sea. It was very dark—reflecting how I still felt inside. Children played on the beach, and for some reason I did not want to go swimming; unusual for me, as I'm generally the first one in the water and the last one out. But this time I had absolutely no desire for pleasurable escapades in the waves.

I nibbled at my food with my fork, lost in thought. I was wondering about my life, about what I was really doing here precisely at this moment, about what my purpose in life really was and why I had followed a stranger to this island. I felt a bit peculiar being here with him in the light of day, this person sitting in front of me whom God had seemingly sent to me and in whom I had total confidence despite my conflicted feelings.

While deep in the flow of my thoughts, I felt his eyes on me.

"Vy you vear sunglasses?" he asked.

"Well, I can't really see without them. My eyes hurt in the sun, don't yours?" I asked back.

"Ven I am here, I don't vant to vear sunglasses. I vant to see the vorld and this magical island vith my own eyes," he said, gesturing with a hand to our surroundings. "I don't vant nothing to interfere vith vat I see and how I see it. Yes?"

"Oh, so you squint all the time," I said, laughing and showing him what squinting meant when he looked confused.

"No, not really," he replied with a serious but tender tone, "your eyes vill get used to the sun, and you vill see the world—the real world—with its real colors, with its real beauty and its real people..." With that, he put his head down and continued to read his newspaper, and I considered the new information he had revealed about himself.

I took off my sunglasses, and the brightness of the sun predictably blinded me, even hurting my eyes. After a minute or two, though, I started to really *feel* my surroundings. My heart ached in my chest. I felt completely bare, like somehow the sunglasses had been protecting me from Artemis's piercing arrows hidden in the sun's rays. Tears started to form and streamed down my face as I looked out unflinchingly at the sea. I quickly wiped them away and pretended that it was only the sun that was making my eyes water. I noticed Ralph scanning me from over the top of his newspaper; I'm sure he knew very well that I was lying, but he must have sensed that I was unwilling to talk about it just yet, and he left it at a glance.

We finished our breakfast and then went for a walk. We didn't talk much; he gave me my space, which I needed. We roamed around the streets, talked to a few people, went for lunch in one of the restaurants in town, and ended with supper in another area on the beach.

"Do you know tavli?" he asked when we came back from the restaurant that evening.

"No, what is that?"

"Vell, it's a game. You vant me to teach you?"

"What kind of game?" I asked, wiggling my eyebrows. Dinner had put me in a better mood, and I felt like joking around a bit with him.

"It is like backgammon, do you know?" he asked.

"Nope, I've never played it before. Teach me?"

"It is a game that you have to think about; it is like a puzzle in a vay," he said while taking out the big, sophisticated-looking wooden case from its green suede pouch.

"Oh...what do you mean, exactly?" I asked, taking out some wine glasses and pouring us a glass.

"Vell, it is like a life puzzle, yes? Everything you do in your life, every decision you make, determines the outcome of it. You have to think about your next move every time, and you have to make sure that each move is good for you. Just like in this game," he said with a little twinkle in his eyes.

"What about when you have no good choices, or others make or have made them for you, and now you have to live with those consequences?" I asked, suddenly feeling defensive.

"Vell...that is a part of your life's puzzle, as vell...I suppose that it is destiny—your destiny. Everyone has their own path to valk, and you have to find your own vay in life. You need to make peace, let go, and move on with your eyes open. Yes?" There was extreme tenderness in his voice.

"Okay, so teach me this game of yours," I replied, changing the subject. I didn't want to keep talking about choice and destiny. I wanted to drink my wine and have fun with my friend—after all, I had a feeling that we'd inevitably circle back to those difficult topics soon enough.

"Okay" he said amiably, understanding that I still did not want to go any deeper.

After he'd taught me the rules of the game, we played nearly every evening for the next month. Sometimes I won; or maybe he just let me win to make me happy. He loved seeing my occasional smiles, which I seldom provided. We played tavli for the next few hours that night, and then went to bed.

River of Tears

The morning arrived, and with it came a disturbing mood that lingered for the rest of the day. I felt very weak and extremely emotionally fragile. I waited awhile before joining Ralph for breakfast since I couldn't stop the river of tears flowing from my eyes. I somehow managed to pull myself together as much as I could and finally got out into the brightness of the sun.

As usual, he was in the middle of his daily routine of sitting at our regular table, having a coffee, smoking a cigarette, and reading his German newspaper. When he saw me, he realized right away that I was not well. He looked at me with his piercing blue eyes, waiting to see if I was going to explain the shape I was in, but I couldn't. I still hadn't found the courage to reveal the reasons behind the emptiness I carried around inside of me.

"I have a surprise for you," he said after a moment or two, recognizing that I was in no mood to open up.

"Thank you, Ralph...what is it?" I asked, relieved to have something to focus on besides my still-watering eyes.

"I vant to take you somvere special today. Ve vill go on a ship to the center of the Caldera. You vil like it, and it vil be good for your soul," he said softly.

We finished our breakfast and drove to the launch area, where a beautiful, tall, wooden sailing ship with a pirate feel to it awaited the tourists. We boarded, sat down on one of the burgundy wooden benches, and watched the beauty of majestic Santorini drift away behind us as we sailed out into the sea. It was a spectacular sight—the houses on top were so tiny and really did look like snow on a mountaintop. I felt so small, both inside and out.

The excursion was magnificent. I did not listen to any of the guide's details about the island, nor did Ralph, as we were in our own little universe. I felt the warm breeze caressing my face, and my eyes feasted on the shadows of the humungous, rocky cliffs around us, their strange facades sculpted by the explosion long ago. It was quite a sight to see alongside the ubiquitous waters of the Mediterranean, which is spectacular on its own, with the deepest shades of blue I've ever seen.

And then there was Ralph. I kept peeking in his direction between glimpses at the scenery. He seemed sad, and kept staring at the captain.

"Do you see him?" he said to me, pointing toward the captain with a head. "I wish sometimes I was like him. Do you see his eyes? They are deep, and he does not say much, but his eyes do. Sometimes it is best to say nothing, let your soul talk for you and the people vill understand you. Ven you are ready...you can talk... I vill listen. Yes?" he said, looking straight through me.

Tears formed anew in my eyes. He gently wiped them off while giving me a, "it's going to be okay" look, then took my hand in his and held it while I put my head on his shoulders. We stayed like that for the rest of the ride while others went out to explore the collapsed volcano. We stayed with the captain, of whom I snapped a photograph for Ralph, who said that he wanted to remember his face and the depth of his eyes. Once the other tourists had come back aboard, the ship continued on around the caldera.

"Thank you, Ralph...I really needed that," I said to him sincerely.

"You are velcome," he said with a simple nod of his head.

"There is a special place I vant to take you next," he added.

"More special places? I don't know if my heart can take more of this," I said, overwhelmed. At the end of the excursion, we took the car and drove to Fira. On the way, he put on some music—a song by Haris Alexiou called *Agapao ki Adiaforo* (I'm in love and I care about nothing).

We parked the car and walked through the tiny, magnificent streets among the white houses and tourist shops at the top of the island.

"Here it is," he said, looking at me with a concerned but hopeful expression.

The restaurant was called Select Café, and it was breathtaking.

Upon entering, your mood is forced to change by the welcoming, soft, peaceful sounds of Enya, Era, Café del Mar, and Enigma, which transport you to another universe. Once the mood is set, you walk to the back of the café, where the magic begins and literally takes your breath away.

The patio is built on the steep, high cliff, all open with dark wooden tables and chairs to match with white seats. The café is surrounded by white houses, hotels, and square-shaped pools that seem to blend seamlessly with the blue horizon.

We sat down, and my heart skipped a beat.

Below us, hundreds of meters down, was the caldera where we had just been a few hours ago. The blinding sun was shining down upon the vast sea, which again created the impression of millions of sparkling stars or diamonds strewn across the surface. Dozens of sailboats, fishing boats, and ships, looking like tiny toys below, bobbed across the gentle waves. Looking out at this spectacular sight, I felt simultaneously like a giant and like I was so insignificantly small that I could disappear on the breeze.

This feeling was bigger than me, and suddenly my "little" problems were only a speck of dust beside this splendor. It was just too much to take in at once—overwhelming and obliterating. Ralph kept watching me, waiting for me to say something, anything. But I was silent, unable to speak even if I had wanted to.

We sat down, and he ordered us some beer while I kept observing the spectacle before me, the melodic music transporting me deep into the part of my heart where my senses came alive—and where I had no choice but to yield to my desires and accept them.

"Ralph...this is so beautiful..." I said, my tears returning once again. "Now I understand why you come here so often. You are right. Santorini is a magical place."

"Santorini is the mother of my heart," he said, affirming what he had told me on the ferry. "Santorini gets inside your heart and never lets go of it. It is here that I come to find peace, and it is here that I find my vay, too," he said with warmth in his blue eyes, looking out at the vast, glittering sea. Again, the sadness crept back into his voice, and I wondered about it not for the first time.

We sat there for hours in silence, understanding that we needed each other in our lives at this precise moment, but not to talk. There was not much to say, really; we were both aware of the magic between us, and he understood the wonder unfolding inside of me as I took in the view— he had felt it years earlier when he'd visited the island for the first time.

We stayed until the sun transformed the horizon again into a gigantic canvas of pinks, reds, and oranges; a delightful feast for the eyes. The spectacular colors of Santorini sunsets really do feel like God's tender hand is behind them, caressing and cracking open your soul at once. All you do is feel: feel your pain, feel another person's heartbeat even though you are not touching, feel your body, feel your heart.

For me, letting myself feel my heart and everything it had bottled up inside of it meant finally facing the heart of a young child, as well. It was a heart full of unanswered questions. Why did God choose me to experience life this way? Why was it written in my destiny that I should suffer as I had? With tears running down my face yet again, this time accompanied by Beethoven's "Moonlight Sonata" drifting on the cooling air, I just kept asking the same questions over and over in my head, wondering how to make peace with it all.

"I think it is time to go," Ralph said, sensing that I was about to explode. He paid the check and we left the café hand in hand and again in silence. He put Klaus Hoffmann on the radio system in the car on the drive home, and my emotional struggles plunged deeper and deeper inside of me. He kept glancing toward me as if to tell me with his eyes that I could start talking whenever I was ready.

We arrived back in Kamari, parked the car, and sat in silence for a couple of minutes.

"Do you mind if we go for a walk on the beach?" I asked finally. He nodded, and we made our way down to the sands. Underneath a huge cliff on a little step where I'd sat down, I had my first meltdown. My heart just couldn't take it anymore—I started bawling. Never had I cried so hard in my life, and never since. The depth of my pain was inexplicable to me at the time, but I knew that I couldn't live with it any longer. Ralph held onto me tightly. I needed to be held, needed to feel safe while I shook apart. After about a half an hour of pure sobbing, I calmed down enough to look him straight in the eye and say, "I'm ready."

And so, I began to reveal the first part of the shadows of my past from Slovakia.

Santorini, In My Angel's Arms Again

The glorious sun was rising over the horizon, and Ralph had listened to me the whole night through. My story was not quite finished yet, but my voice had become hoarse and brittle. My eyes were puffy from crying, and I was exhausted—more emotionally than physically. I just wanted to lay my head on a pillow and surrender to the arms of Morpheus.

Ralph, however, had other plans, and although he had no answers or comments about what he had heard, he said, "I know you are tired, but how about ve go for breakfast, take a break, and vatch the rest of the sun rise, and then you can rest. You can continue another time, yes?" I had a difficult time making sense of his words after the long night, but his eyes spoke to me; they spoke of compassion and of pure sadness for what I had trusted him with.

How can a human being sustain this much pain, I thought. How could *he*, still essentially a stranger, make it better? And yet he did—his presence, his aura, his absolute devotion to not just listening but *hearing* my story somehow made it okay for me to grieve and not feel guilty about it. He made me realize that it was okay to cry and to exteriorize the depths of my sorrow. Slowly, he was freeing me from the shadows of my past and forcing me to face them head-on.

We got up and walked to a restaurant that was just opening up and had breakfast by the sea, watching the orange sunrise unfolding before us. After, I went to the edge of the water by myself to regain control of my emotions. At that moment, he snapped a picture of me. This image is one that became quite significant for me, as it vividly captured what was happening inside me. The picture is a shadow of my form emerging from the bright, beautiful sunrise, and it reminds me that even in the harshness of life, there can be and always will be a beautiful light to guide you if you are open to it.

As I watched the spectacle before me, I was overwhelmed with joy—yes, joy. It was a strange feeling to have after such an exhausting night. Yet I still had much more to say, and still more healing to do. It took about a week for me to be able to release my entire story.

One evening while playing tavli, a couple of days following my first unburdening, I shared with Ralph my desire to go on my own to Paros. Paros is one of my favorite islands where I spent many happy summers with my mother, the memories of which are firmly anchored in my heart. He agreed that it was a good idea, and the next day I was off. But what I thought I desired the previous evening evaporated when I ended up alone on the ship.

I couldn't put my finger on what was happening. The adventurer inside me seemed to have been put on temporary hold during my healing process with my German angel. I arrived in Paros confused, shattered, and with a whole lot of mixed emotions swirling around inside me. This sense of unease and befuddlement was so new to me; I was usually a very confident person who was always excited about thrilling new adventures. However, this journey was one of healing, and healing is sometimes confusing and difficult.

I decided to stay the rest of the day and night and leave the next day. My years of experience as a traveler put me in autopilot mode immediately, and I did what I needed to do, which was find a room, get something to eat, and find a phone. I remembered a little B&B from the pier by the church from my numerous previous visits.

I went to see the owner, and oddly enough, he remembered me and gave me a cute little room to stay in for the night. I put my backpack down—I've learned through the years not to travel heavy, and I could fit everything I needed for a month in a regular-size backpack. I went on to call Ralph, and since I'd been to Paros so many times, my instincts and the familiarity of the streets guided me to a phone.

"Hi, Ralph. I miss you so much! What the heck am I doing here, anyway? I should be with you. I want to be in Santorini with you back at Select Café. I am so confused, and I feel like my heart has been torn into pieces. I took a room for tonight, but I am going back tomorrow; come and pick me up, okay?" I said to him, my voice shaking.

"Calm down, C.C., I miss you too. I miss you so much... My Canadian Sunshine, I too vant to see you; if you vant to leave, of course I vill pick you up, but I think it is good for you to stay for the night, yes?" he said to me as softly as he could. With heavy hearts, we said our good-byes and hung up. Even this small thing was enormously difficult for me. Looking back, it seems almost pitifully funny—we were seeing each other the next day, after all.

My mood lightened slightly as I walked along the delightful pier, went for a beer in the most popular taverna, and strolled to my favorite place to rent a mopette. I'd spent many days around this area with my good friend Micky from Thessaloniki—who had worked at the mopette shop—years earlier. The shop always had good prices for the little motored bikes, although over the years and with the advent of the euro, the prices have gone through the roof.

I proudly hopped on my mopette, and off I went to my favorite spots on the island, listening to Klaus Hoffmann with the soft, warm breeze caressing my face and carrying with it the inebriating aromas of thyme and lavender.

I visited Naousa, Piso Livadi, Lefkes, and Kostos, where I took a bite to eat, and then I headed out to

Pounda Beach where I stopped to watch a football game between Brazil and Turkey. The beach is a young person's paradise filled with laughter, happy screams, cheers, and deafening music that I'm not a fan of but the younger islanders seemed to greatly enjoy.

Continuing on my circuit, I pit-stopped by Golden Beach and Santa Sofia, where I found my old beach had transformed as much as I had. Sand now covered a gorgeous wading pool where I used to lie for hours. It was still a magnificent place to spend quality time with yourself. I finally completed my tour at Parasporos, where my mother and I had camped and had an unforgettable time meeting the most exceptionally original people in the world.

After my ride, I returned the mopette and headed back to my room, where I spent the rest of the day listening to music and writing in my journal. I couldn't wait to get back to my German angel's serene presence. I felt silly being there on my own, which I usually yearned for, but this was no usual adventure. I fell asleep that night with tears in my eyes yet again, hoping for some kind of enlightenment.

I woke up to a knock at the door; it was my host, delivering my much-needed breakfast of bread with jam and some coffee. As I said my goodbyes to my kind host, he said something strange to me.

"Good luck for your next chapter, C.C..." It was as if he knew exactly what I was going through; or perhaps he had just seen many lost souls like me, passing through his charming little B&B like a doorway from one stage of one's life to another.

Even though my short excursion had been beautiful, I still left Paros with a mixture of disappointment, emptiness, and dissatisfaction inside of me. I was just too eager to see Ralph again; I yearned to reveal the rest of my story to this extraordinary man. Now that I'd begun to unburden myself, I wanted it all out in the open where I could finally examine it in the light of day and then— hopefully—release it into her majesty the Mediterranean, where it could be washed away for good.

The beauty and uniqueness of Santorini slowly came into sight as my boat drew closer and closer. My heart was pounding in my eagerness to see Ralph again. I disembarked, and there he was, my beautiful blue-eyed angel, that peculiar, subtle ghost of a smile on his lips and his arms wide open for me. I felt like I had come home.

"I missed you so much, Ralph!" I said, falling into his outstretched arms.

"Oh, my Canadian Sunshine, I missed you, too. Vat are ve going to do?" I knew very well the meaning behind those words. How exactly are we going to say goodbye to each other eventually after these weeks together? But I said nothing. I didn't want to think about that, not now; it was too painful to conceive.

After a long embrace, we walked together hand in hand and sat down at the pier's restaurant for a beer. It was becoming a habit of ours—holding hands—and it was like a stream of energy between us that we couldn't comprehend but accepted nonetheless. This was the nature of our nonsexual relationship; forged between two souls who needed each other in this moment in time. It was like a part of me was missing when I was away from him. I just couldn't explain it. I believe now that he had been sent to me by a higher power, which is why I called him my angel.

Let the Healing Begin

We spent the early morning the next day at the restaurant with his Yugoslavian friend.

"Time to go, yes?" he said after a while, his piercing eyes fixing me with a knowing stare.

"Yes!" I said, understanding very well that he wanted to take me back to Select Café as my welcome-home present. "I missed this so much," I said with enthusiasm.

We set off in his car, listening to Klaus Hoffmann's instrumental "Afghana", *Café del Mar vol. 9*, and Haris Alexiou's *Psithiroi* album; music that reflected the spirit we were in. We arrived in Fira, parked the car, and walked once more through the charming, narrow streets that led to Select Café where "the hand of God," as Ralph would regularly say, was awaiting our arrival.

We sat down at our usual table, contemplating the humbling, heart-stopping scenery while we chitchatted about my trip.

"Stay here, I vill be back soon," he said to me all of a sudden. I nodded, and off he went, disappearing into the crowd. I got lost again in the beauty of my surroundings, my thoughts fixed on the next chapter of my existence, whatever that might hold. How was I going to tell him about the confusion with my sister over a decade ago? What to say about that? What about everything else that I was still carrying around?

I was writing in my journal when he came back to the table, sat down, and handed me a small, delicately wrapped box on top of an envelope. I looked at him with a question in my eyes.

"What is this?" I asked, puzzled.

"This is for you, open it," he said with a mixture of pride and nervousness. I opened the box, and inside was a very elegant yellow ring. Inside the yellow ring was another ring made of white gold that turned in the yellow ring's orbit. I was completely speechless.

"Ven you vill be lost in this crazy vorld, just turn this ring and you vill find your vay. The right vay, the vay for you, and the vorld will not be so hard anymore. You vill understand that vere you are is exactly vere you are supposed to be at this precise time. You vill think about this time here in Santorini, and it vill all make sense again. You must find your vey, C.C.," he said to me in his soft voice while watching my stunned expression.

I noticed right away that he wore a brand-new ring just like the one he had bought me on his finger.

"I want *your* ring, Ralph," I said impulsively. "I want yours because it makes more sense for me to have yours. You will forever be with me then, and when I turn your ring, all this—" I gestured to our surroundings "—will make even more sense to me. It will be a never-ending memory of us, of what and how I should live my life."

"I vill give it to you at the end of our journey. Until then I vill fill it with my energy," he said with a genuine smile. I opened his letter then, the specifics of which I will keep to myself, but it talked about my chaotic, drastic entrance into his life and about not knowing how we would ever be able to say our goodbyes.

"Oh, Ralph...I don't know what else to tell you but thank you! Thank you for taking me here. You have shown me so much compassion, and I don't know what will become of us after this trip. I don't want to think about the time when we will have to part. I know you told me I have to find my way, and that is what I will be doing when I leave you, but I just...I just can't think about that time yet. I love you very much. I have grown with you. This is an escape, a passing through that we both needed, I guess. You will forever be imbedded in my heart, and I am grateful for this time with you. Thank you for this ring, I will cherish it and wear it with pride and understanding as I continue to discover my way in this world." At this point I had started to cry, humbled as I was by his selfless generosity.

We looked at each other with a new understanding of our situation. I was supposed to be happy, but I was also torn inside between him and the necessity of continuing my life elsewhere, wherever that might be—and there was still so much I needed to face before I could do that. As I watched him, his eyes gave me a glimpse of the injured soul hidden deep within him; a no-man's-land that I couldn't even begin to comprehend.

"There is beauty in this vorld, you know, and ve are sitting in the middle of it," Ralph said. "You need to let go and understand that you and only you can find your vay...alone. I am just a passenger in your path, trying to guide you and to help you understand that you are vorth much more than you think, and that you can have faith in vat is to come. You cannot blame your unhappiness on others; you have to figure out your own puzzle. I am not the man for you...nor is Gigi for that matter, because ve vere there to help "teach" you your vorth, and just like a patient cannot be with his doctor, our destiny is not to be together. You must find your vay, C.C. Your past is part of who you are, and it is up to you to accept it."

He said all of this very diplomatically, seemingly un-sure of his last words. I knew very well the truth behind what he was saying, but I just couldn't process it in that moment. My heart was aching, and I just wanted to shout out loud and throw myself into his arms. But I didn't. I sat there with tears streaming down my face, both of us lost in this moment in time that we would never forget. This was monumental—this was bigger than both us. It was clear that we were both on different journeys, but that in meeting each other our lives would be transformed, helping us to become the people we were meant to be.

We turned our heads toward the splendid view, and I was overwhelmed by my memories again. He looked at me, and I knew it was a welcoming gesture to start where I had left off with my tale. And so I began to tell him about my life in Montreal.

Select Café, Santorini

Once more, I emptied the tears from my soul, and once more he listened to me, speechless—for now. By the time I had divulged this new chapter of my life, the sun had disappeared over the caldera, and from this magnificent crepuscule emerged the incandescent nighttime dance of our surroundings. From the twinkling lights of the ships below to the beautifully decorated hotel balconies, everything sparkled and glowed.

No one cared much for us staying for such a ridiculously long time. I think that the café staff were used to people from every corner of the planet lingering, however, drawn as everyone was to this mystical, sacred place to do exactly what I was doing: renewing their faith in their own lives and shaking off the shadows of their past.

The more I emptied myself of these horrible memories, the lighter I felt. I was reliving each one as I spoke, and Ralph really listened as I did so, waiting for the appropriate moment to speak or give advice.

"That is a lot, isn't it?" he said to me, saddened and compassionate but never piteous.

"Yes it is, and I carry these feelings and flashbacks with me wherever I go, and I don't know how to make peace with it all, you know?"

"You need to really understand that all this, first of all, vas not your fault," Ralph continued. "Yes, you had it vorse than many, but this is not who you are. You have to go on your path with your eyes vide open, be more subtle in your vays, and throw your sadness in the sea. Your past does not define your future. It vas your destiny to come here, and someone up there chose you because you are strong, because you have a heart of gold. And you gave me so much, too. You taught me about love, you opened my own heart, and you have complicated my life in so many vays." By the time he had finished telling me all of this, he had a hint of a smile on his face. "Come, let's go home. Tomorrow is a new day, yes?"

In the days that followed, I seemed to be breathing much better. A smile had formed on my lips, and I somehow felt freer, like this huge weight had been lifted from my soul. I was starting to become a new version of me, a happier, stronger individual with a drive to propel myself into a new chapter of my life.

From that day on, there were no more episodes of heart-rending stories; it was me and him, healing alongside each other in our own ways, at peace in the land of the gods. I had cried all of my tears, and now they were one with the majestic Mediterranean that surrounded us. I didn't talk about my past anymore—not because I didn't want to, but because I didn't need to.

One day at the breakfast table, Ralph said, "We vill have to go to Athens in a couple of days, yes?"

"Oh, okay, for what?" I asked, a bit puzzled. Why would we need to leave Santorini?

"I have to see some people there for my business in Germany," he replied.

"What kind of business?" I asked around a bite of breakfast; the subject had somehow never come up.

"I have a store with Greek artifacts, and I need to get some more stuff for it. You vill come and help me choose, yes?" he said, always in his serious tone of voice that I had become accustomed to. He took out some pictures of his store and showed them to me. It was very elegant and clean-looking.

"Okay Ralph, I would love to do that, and since I speak a bit of Greek, I can let you know if they are taking you for a ride," I said with a smile.

"Vat do you mean? I don't understand," he asked seriously.

"Oh, I forgot that you don't understand some expressions...well, what I mean is that I will be your *spy* and see if they are going to try to take more money from you than they should. If they will lie to you, understand?" I explained to him.

"Yes, I understand now," he said, a hint of a smile peeking out from behind his raised coffee cup. "Ve vill make a good team. Ven ve get to Athens, I vant you to call your sister, as well. You need to talk to her and try to fix things up with her. And I vant her to see who I am so that she is not vorried, yes?"

"Oh...I don't know, Ralph. We are having such a wonderful time...do I have to get back into the past again so soon?" I asked, reluctant to face the idea of a family reunion.

"Yes! You only have one sister. I know you love her very much, and I think that you need to spend some time vit her. She needs to see that you are vell and that I have not mistreated you, and she needs to meet me. That vay, she vill know that you are safe, and after all, you are here for this purpose—to confront things you othervise vould not. Yes? I think that it vill be good for both of you," he said, leaning forward in emphasis.

"Okay, Ralph, I know you are right. Thank you," I said. The more I thought about it, the more I liked the idea. I missed her, and she must have been a little worried about me by now. In her eyes, I was probably on a free-for-all of pure partying. Little did she know that this man was freeing me slowly from my horrors and bombarding me with a new kind of understanding of my pure worth.

I was actually getting quite nervous when Friday arrived and we were on our way with the car hauled into the belly of the ferry.

"Don't be afraid, C.C.," Ralph said to me calmly, sensing my nerves. "I just vant her to see that you are okay—more than okay—and I vant you to talk to her," he added.

"I know, I know, Ralph, but I just don't know what to tell her," I said, searching for answers in his steady eyes.

"You vill find the right vords ven you see her," he said reassuringly.

As we sailed off, I thought about how I would eventually need to face the reality of my situation, and my relationship with my sister was as good a place to start as any. But for now, we were on a temporary break from these looming responsibilities. I let myself get lost in the lull of the ferry's engines, safe by Ralph's side.

A Mini-Vacation

We arrived in Athens and went straight to our hotel to freshen up. He called some friends of his to find out where we would meet later on for supper.

"Today ve are going to have fun with my friends, yes?" he said with his small smile. "And you vill be the person who you truly are. There is no more need for you to be sad, C.C.—all of that is gone. You are strong, and you have to learn to love yourself the vay you are. Think of your past now as a blessing, not a curse, because you are my Canadian Sunshine. Yes?"

"Yes!" I said. I was becoming stronger and much more confident than the woman he had met just a few short weeks earlier. I was feeling more like the woman I wanted to be.

We strolled through the crowded streets of smoggy, noisy Athens and ended up in a typical Greek taverna café for lunch. We then headed off to visit many whole-salers in search of artifacts for Ralph's shop. I pointed out the ones I liked, and he bought them. When we were finished, we packed the car full of his new goodies and went back to get ready for the evening.

We arrived at a beautiful outdoor restaurant with trees and glittering Christmas lights surrounding the property. The tables were set out on the grass, and one was already full of his friends. That evening, I discovered that my Ralph was not only compassionate with me, but with others as well. He always seemed to be there for you one hundred percent, no matter what. When he looked at you, he really *looked* at you. He listened to everyone with that small smile on his face, and I think that I saw him laugh—really laugh, as in a my-belly-hurts kind of laugh—for the first time since our journey began. I must admit, it was a breath of fresh air. We had so much fun that night; we laughed, ate, drank, and I think that we even danced, although he had absolutely no rhythm from what I remember.

The next day, we set off again to tour the wholesalers for additional merchandise. We were in the middle of looking through some wares when he gave me his phone and told me to call my sister to see where to meet up with her later on that evening. She lived about an hour away, and we made a reservation at a restaurant we both knew where we had eaten before years ago. I was quite appre-hensive of how this whole situation would unfold.

We arrived at the restaurant early, so we sat down and waited for her to arrive.

"You vill be fine," Ralph reassured me tenderly. "You vill make things good vit the only sister you have, yes?" I just nodded nervously.

I finally saw her walk in, and what a beautiful woman she was. Heads turned as she walked through the restaurant—tall, gorgeous, slim, and elegant, there was no ignoring her presence. As she approached us, I remembered all our times spent together in the land of the gods, all the places she took me to, the laughs we had, and how I sometimes gave her grief because I just wanted to be on my own, my restless spirit always pulling at its tethers. In that moment I realized how much I'd missed her.

We hugged, and I proudly presented her to Ralph. She looked at him with suspicion, and she greeted him a bit coldly, clearly wary of this stranger who had whisked her little sister off to the islands.

"Hi, my name is Ralph," he said, giving her a polite smile. "It is nice to meet you. C.C. is staying vit me in Santorini."

"Hi, I am Maya, C.C.'s sister. Nice to meet you, too. I hope you are taking good care of her. Can I see your driver's license, please? I want to make sure you are who you say you are," she said, her expression still cold. I tried not to roll my eyes.

I thought she was being overly aggressive, but Ralph handed over his papers as if this was the most natural thing in the world to ask for.

"Don't vorry, I am not a monster. I am taking care of C.C. and we are okay, I just vanted you to know that," he said. "Now I am leaving you. I vill be right there in the other restaurant ven you are finished, so you just let me know and I am going to pick you up, yes?" he added, looking straight at me and letting me know with his eyes that I could tell him that I wanted to leave, and we would. With that, he was gone.

We sat down and began to talk.

"Ralph wanted you to see for yourself that I am alive and well," I said reassuringly.

"Well, I was wondering. How are you, really, C.C.? Are you well? Are you having a good time? Is he good to you? German, hum?" she said, a hint of a smile on her face.

"Yes, everything is okay. More than okay, actually," I answered. Her smile grew wider—she must have seen how genuinely at peace I seemed—and the conversation developed easily from there.

By the time we were done, two hours had passed. I had given Ralph the sign that all was okay, and that it was time to go.

"Take good care of my sister," Maya said again to Ralph, but this time with a smile instead of a cold appraisal. "But I see that you are doing a good job of that already."

And just like that, this special moment in time passed as quickly as everything else. I had gained a new trust with my sister, and had freed my heart a little more. To say that we would become best friends would be a lie, and there was still much to talk about, but we had forged a new beginning together, and I owe it all to my blue-eyed angel.

We hugged and said our goodbyes; she was going back to her life and Ralph and I back to our temporary paradise.

"How do you feel?" he asked me. I knew that he wouldn't push me on details, for which I was grateful.

"I feel good, Ralph," I said. "Again, thank you. Thank you for insisting on me seeing her. I feel good about us now." Again I felt like crying, but this time, the tears had no time to tumble down my cheeks; they disappeared as soon as they surfaced.

It was a beautiful evening. We set off to the tunes of Enya, Klaus Hoffmann, and Haris Alexiou. I was becoming more and more accustomed to the underlying meaning of these songs I found so much comfort in. They had become our constant companions, and they started to impact my thoughts and emotions through their deep meanings.

We drove to Pireas and waited for our ferry. I was thinking about the inevitable point when my time with Ralph would come to an end—these were frightening thoughts for me. How could I leave this man, and how would I survive the heartache? But for now I was grateful that we still had two more weeks to enjoy each other's company, and in a better frame of mind this time.

Our Haven Awaits

We arrived in the early morning on our magical island and headed straight to his Albanian friend's café, where we stayed for a while.

"How nice it is to be back home," I said joyfully.

"Yes, it is," he answered, sadness creeping into his eyes.

"What's wrong?" I asked.

"I never told you, but I lost my father. I have a big hole in my heart now. He vas very important to me, and I never recovered from it." He paused for a moment before speaking again, as recovering from this admission. "And then you came...my beautiful Canadian Sunshine. You came and gave me hope for a better time in my life. You say that I gave you so much in yours, but if you only knew how much you have given me in mine. You gave me my heart back. I never thought I could feel love again, and you are making my life very complicated right now, cause I don't know vat to do. If only ve had met at another time, I vould not let you leave back to Canada," he said with something of a smirk, although his eyes were still sad.

"You are a very strong person, you need to under-stand that," he continued, "and you need to go your own vay without the hurt from your past, like I do, in a vay. You need to find your dreams and make them come true. Look at the beauty around you. You also make people happy, ven you are not crying," he added with his unique smile. "You are one special voman, and you vill do good things, and I hope one day I vill get an email from you telling me that you have found your vay in the vorld."

I didn't know what to tell him; I was in no position to give him any advice, as I still felt like I was the student in this relationship, so I just sat there, taking him in and holding his hand. I hoped that my eyes conveyed every-thing that I couldn't put into words. We stayed like that for a while, staring at each other as the din of everyday life at the pier bustled around us.

A few days later, we were invited for dinner with some of his friends on another part of the island. We got ready, but there was something in the air that night; something that we didn't need to express in words. We arrived, were greeted ever so kindly, and I was introduced to his friends. It was a pleasant evening.

We drank ouzo and had a nice supper. The whole eve-ning we kept staring at each other, knowing very well that these wonderful times were coming to an end soon for us, and the pain that we felt from this inevitability was quite evident on our faces. We didn't need to voice our fears to each other; we felt them, just like you feel the sun's heat on your skin or the stinging cut from a sharp knife.

We went to bed that night without a single word spoken, deep in our thoughts.

In the days that followed, the atmosphere lightened, and we played tavli on our balcony just like we had nearly every day, accompanied by a glass of wine. We went to Fira, and just enjoyed each other's company without saying a word about our upcoming goodbye.

The following weekend we were off again to Athens for another shopping spree for his store. I didn't meet up with my sister this time. That weekend, however, it started to pour like cats and dogs, as the expression goes. The rain seemed like the Greek gods had heard my cries, felt my pain, and decided to join in on the tears that I'd wept in Santorini.

The tremendous amount of rain that poured from the sky flooded the streets and created rivers right before our eyes, and we were stuck in the middle of it. Rushing streams flowed where streets were supposed to be, soon gushing into the stores. We hid in one of the stores, the water up to our knees, and ended up helping the owners with mucking the water back out. We all passed bucket after bucket filled with water to each other, trying to empty the store as quickly as possible.

The rain subsided after a while, and the flow of the water from the streets, just like the tears I had wept on our sacred island, vanished. I was astonished at the metaphorical relevance of this event. As we watched the rest of the water drain away, I somehow understood that the massive surge of pain and sorrow I'd cried out over the past few weeks was forever gone, and that flowers of peace now arose from where those tears had fallen. My life would be filled with new memories now—ones that didn't require tears.

We set off once more on the ferry to Santorini at the end of the weekend of rain and revelations. This was our last week together.

The End of a Beautiful Love Affair

We came back once again to Santorini to spend our last days together. We did exactly as we had been for the past four weeks: eating our breakfast at the Splash Bar in the mornings, where Ralph always waited for me, newspaper in hand, and then watching the ships unloading newcomers at the pier at his Albanian friend's restaurant. The amount of hours we spent there will forever be embedded in my memories; the simple joys of watching life go by and enjoying each other's company.

We loved to people-watch. It had become a game for us to wonder which ones were visiting our magical island haven for which reasons. Perhaps some have felt the same way about the island as I felt. Perhaps some were there doing exactly what I had been doing. And who knows, perhaps someone even met their own angel along the way.

Every day of that last week, we spent every minute we could at the Select Café; tearless on my part this time, thank God! Sadness slowly overcame us, and we spoke less and less of our inevitable parting. Even though I felt free from the restoration of harmony in my life, with a brand-new light at the end of the tunnel, new, unnerving feelings were also emerging, and I was extremely fearful of leaving Ralph and of being left to fend for myself once more.

"You know that you can call me anytime if you need anything," he said reassuringly while we sat together at Select Café a few days before our departure.

"Yes, I know, but Ralph, what am I going to do without you?" I said, trying and failing to hide my distress.

"Remember, you need to find your vay, C.C.," he said firmly. "Remember to look ahead, to never look back, and to always keep your eyes open. Now you are free, you know who you are...and that is a strong person, who doesn't pity herself," he continued.

"Yes, I know. I am quite proud of myself, actually. This has been quite an adventure, I must say, Ralph," I said with a hint of a smile, which he returned.

"You should be proud, and yes, it has been a vonderful time. My Canadian Sunshine is ready to face to vorld with new eyes now, yes?" I nodded, and then he got up from his chair. "Vait here," he said, "and I vill be back in a few minutes."

"Okay, I'm not going nowhere," I said teasingly.

I was lost in my thoughts when he sat down in front of me again and deposited a gift bag on the table.

"Here you go," he said, obviously quite proud of himself.

"What is this? Is it for me?" I asked with humor, knowing by the glimmer in his eyes that the package was for me.

"Open it."

I unwrapped the gift bag carefully, and inside was a beautifully hand-painted view of Santorini on a hard-cover notebook. I was speechless. He knew how much I loved to write.

"This is so you can vrite the new chapters of your life," he said kindly while handing me another gift bag; a bit bigger this time. "But I have something else too for you. Open it, please," he said, gesturing to the bag.

I unwrapped the new present, and inside it was a small cream-colored bag with a small pocket on the outside, again with a painting of Santorini on its side.

"And this is for the new luggage in your life; for your new vay, ven you find it," he said with a smirk.

"Thank you, Ralph. Again, you never cease to surprise me with the many gifts that you have given me. Do you know how much I will miss you, and how much you helped me in my life?" I said, tearing up again for what felt like the hundredth time, but this time they were tears of happiness.

"I have given you nothing that you didn't already have in yourself. It is you who have given me so much heart; you made me open myself up once more, and I vill be ever grateful for that," he said, the truth and intensity of his words striking my heart.

I knew he was right; these five weeks had given me more peace and harmony than any of my previous travels had. I hadn't know what to expect, but I was so glad in that moment that I had decided to go with him that day on the ferry.

I think that what Ralph meant by "finding my vay" was that I should find happiness in whatever I was to do in my life; to not escape anymore through my travels, but instead to really enjoy my surroundings fully wherever I found myself, free of the pain of my past. And this was something I could finally do. I was no longer a message in a bottle being tossed around by the waves of a tempestuous sea. I was taking the reins of my destiny, holding my head up high, and moving forward regardless of the bumpy road behind me. In saying that I needed to now find my way, Ralph was telling me that there was absolutely no reason for me not to be fulfilled and to lead a happy life now. And he was right.

Sitting at the café with him, holding my beautiful journal and bag, I realized that it wasn't as much of what he had said to me that had helped me, but more that he had given me the time to speak and the opportunity to heal in a magical sanctuary where I wouldn't be judged for processing my grief. I'd not only opened my Pandora's Box—I'd dumped its entire contents into the glorious vastness of the Mediterranean.

I only then understood how strong I was, never having relied on drugs or alcohol to soothe my pain. I also realized that it was time for us to part so that I could propel myself into beautiful new chapters of my life, stronger than ever. I understood that all of those events in my life had happened for a reason, difficult as they were. I realized that I had an opportunity to share my story with the world, especially with struggling souls like myself, so that they might realize that turning to drugs, alcohol, resentment, anger, denial, self-pity, and worst, suicide, is not an option nor a solution. You cannot change your past, but you have the capacity to change your future by believing in and following your destiny, by listening to that little voice inside of you that guides you—and by sometimes letting angels enter your life when you need them the most.

I came to accept my past with harmony, and in a peculiar way, to even be proud of it. It was my path, my story, however winding and sometimes broken. A higher power decided that I was strong enough to sustain these hardships and to use me to convey the message that whatever happens to you is part of your destiny's path—the good and the bad. Whatever we are going through, we are strong enough to bear it, because we've been chosen to experience our lives exactly as they are.

Once I understood this and accepted this as my fate, I really did grow to love my life in all its intricacy. My life forged me into the complex and original person I am now, and I wouldn't change that.

Today, I thanked my father over the phone for the decision he made over thirty years ago to kidnap me. It was an egotistical, selfish, and cruel decision that altered lives of so many. However, in doing so, he gave me a chance at a new life. I did let him know that his actions toward my mother had wounded me deeply, even though I've learned to accept even that as part of my destiny's path.

Some were surprised that I'd forgiven him. The reasoning behind my clemency is actually very selfish. I did it for me. I understood that if I had kept the hatred within my soul, it would have destroyed my life. So I released the pain and transferred it into humbling acceptance of the events of my past. I also did it for my future children; I wanted to be a good mother, and I knew that I couldn't do this with such a heavy weight still sitting on my heart.

By firmly and purely deciding that the events of my past weren't going to consume or affect my future life, I freed myself from feeling guilty. Staring in the mirror, I had to repeat dozens of times to the reflection of a young woman who desperately needed to hear these magical words out loud: "It wasn't your fault." None of it was.

I wasn't going to become a casualty of my own life's path.

I knew that my happiness relied solely on how I interpreted the events on my journey. So I chose to see those events for what they actually were: just my life! My wonderful, crazy, fascinating life.

Although my father will never admit to the abuse he visited on my mother, nor to the fact that he took me for any other reason than "love," I think that, as time had passed, he has learned to love me genuinely and in his own peculiar way.

I could have ended up on a completely opposite path of self-destruction and endless pain, but I chose to face my life head-on...with a little help from a German angel.

Poignant Goodbyes

The time had come for us to pack our bags and say goodbye—goodbye to Santorini, to each other, to these magical five weeks we'd spent in each other's company.

The apartment, which had also become our home, would soon become a new home for the brand-new beginnings of someone else's journey. Although our destinies had been momentarily and inexorably entwined, they were now parting ways again. Healing had been done on both of our parts, my Pandora's Box had been put to rest, and harmony had been restored. Although I was deeply saddened by our parting, I was also excited that new chapters were about to be written in my notebook.

We sat in the car, and one last time said goodbye to our home, which was disappearing behind us as we headed for the pier. As we watched Kamari disappear in the rearview mirrors, our hearts grew heavy with the many memories that had transformed our lives over the past few weeks. This was it; there was no turning back, and we had to face the reality of parting from each other. When we reached the pier, we sat at the little restaurant where we had spent oh —so- many sweet hours together and waited until the last moment to board the ferry. We parked the car and headed for the deck so that we could say goodbye to our spectacular island.

We held each other like our lives depended on it— motionless, speechless, and with tears in our eyes, waiting for the ferry to take us to our new beginnings and separate paths. As the horns tore through the air, letting everyone know that it was time to go, we held each other even closer. We watched our hand of God slowly disappearing before us, our hearts ever heavier. Our unique story of love and chance and healing would forever be engraved upon the island and our souls alike, and I would be forever grateful for our time together.

Throughout the journey to Piraeus, words were scarce; neither of us knew how to put words to what we were feeling, or to the enormity of what we had shared for the past five weeks. The scenery began to reveal that we were getting closer to the inevitable. We arrived sooner than I would have liked, and with a pounding heart in my chest and tears slowly making their way down my cheeks, I contemplated where my path would lead me next. Where would I find the strength to shake it off? No, not my past—that part was done—but rather the pain of letting go of my German angel. I knew without a shadow of a doubt that I was well equipped to face the next chapters of my life, but leaving the man who had made this possible was another matter entirely.

We disembarked from the ferry and headed straight for a restaurant at the pier. I wasn't very hungry, but we tried to stretch our remaining time together as much as we could. The dreadful moment inevitably arrived, and it was time to go. We needed to part so that I could walk the rest of my journey on my own and deal with the secondary portion of my healing. I knew this; I knew I had to do the rest on my own, but for now, I was much too absorbed by the wretchedness of goodbye.

"It's time to go, C.C. I must be on my vay, and you must continue on your own. You know that you can always count on me. Call me if you need any money, or if you need anything else. Remember, you are strong," he said reassuringly, but he was trembling. "How about ve meet every year in June in Bari on the deck of the Superfast and go together to Santorini. Yes?" he continued, smiling at me with his sweet semi-smile.

Even though I knew it would be a miracle if I could pull that off, I responded with an enthusiastic nod.

"That would be amazing. Yes, let's make a rendezvous for next year. Same time, same place, same ferry? Then we will be together again," I said through my tears. We both knew that we were speaking of something that had a very slim chance of becoming a reality, but it served to lighten the heavy mood a bit and let us pretend for a sweet moment that we could continue to be a part of each other's lives.

"Good," he said, that smile that I had grown to love so much over the last five weeks still on his lips.

We walked hesitantly to the car one last time together, delaying as long as possible. We listened to our favorite song, Klaus Hoffmann's, "Come Let's ride the Wind", for the short drive to a more isolated part of the pier where we would part for good.

With the song fading, he slowly stopped the car. We got out and embraced—an embrace filled with the mixed emotions of sorrow, joy, gratitude, melancholy, and wonder at our unknown futures apart. I tried not to let these challenging feelings keep me from remembering that I had to throw him back in the ocean so that I could move on and so he could perhaps help other lost souls like myself. I was so grateful to the universe for sending me this angel of a man to carry my broken soul in his hands for a while. He was on his way and I was on mine; this was it.

"I have one last gift for you, vait..." he said, opening the door to his car and taking the mini stereo from the back seat, which we'd used throughout our five weeks together while playing Tavli in the evenings.

"This is so you can listen to our favorite songs and remember who you really are. It vill keep you company for the next part of your journey, yes?" he said tenderly, never giving me a chance to respond, although I couldn't have responded in that moment anyway.

"Goodbye, my Canadian Sunshine...find your vay and come back to me next year vit many new vonderful chapters in your new notebook, yes?"

He slowly took off his ring and placed it on my finger.

"Yes...Yes, I will," I managed. "Goodbye, my German angel. You will forever be in my heart." I took off my ring and tenderly placed it on his little finger. We looked at each other for a long time then, our eyes saying everything that we could not say with words, which was the way in which we communicated best, anyway. We hugged tightly one last time, tears on both of our faces.

"See you next year."

We reluctantly let go of each other. He walked to the trunk, opened it, took out my backpack, and set it gracefully on the ground beside me. Giving me one last quick, tight hug, he then walked slowly back to the car, his head down. He started the car, turned on our favorite song, put the car into gear, looked at me once more with his beautiful blue eyes, and drove away into the morning traffic.

Just like that, he was gone. If my life were a Hollywood movie, he would have come racing back to me, but no—this was really the end. The despair I felt was too much to bear, so I sat down on the edge of the water and emptied out the last of my tears into the ocean. But these were not the same type of tears of desolation and hopelessness that I had experienced during out time in Santorini; no, these were just regular, good old-fashioned tears. I had been freed, lightened, and although I hated to see Ralph go that day, inside me was a new sense of eagerness in following my new path.

After I'd had time to process our last moments together and cry my last tears, I pulled myself together, gave myself a little pep talk, brushed myself off and wiped the tears from my cheeks, replacing them with a smile. I wanted to reflect the gratitude I felt inside on the outside. I wanted to celebrate and grieve no more. I felt lucky in every aspect of my tumultuous life, which now would be filled with the wonderful new experiences that I knew awaited me. This time, I would be running toward adventure instead of away from my demons.

I collected my belongings, put my backpack on, and with my smile still beaming, I grabbed the ghetto blaster in my right hand and began walking toward my future.

Conclusion

With the help of my German angel on our enchanting island of Santorini, I had freed myself from the ghosts of my past and was now being propelled into a new, fulfilling life where I traveled for pure pleasure, not escape.

By accepting people like Ralph and Gigi into my life and allowing myself to be completely vulnerable in their presence and life lessons, a wonderful thing had happened: a gate leading to forgiveness had swung open in all aspects of my life—both toward the people who had wounded me deeply as well as toward myself. By accepting the events of my life as my fate and by simply deciding that those events were not this enormous, insurmountable mountain that I couldn't conquer, it became an easy task for me to think and talk about them without any hint of animosity. I saw my past as a part of a greater destiny, not as wounds that couldn't be healed. From the moment I decided to see my life this way, everything unfolded exactly as I wanted it to for the simple reason that I was open to it with freedom.

By watching *The Secret* a decade later and adopting its teachings, I deepened my belief in my self-worth. As part of concluding my healing process, I wrote a long letter to my father as well as to all the people who had wronged and abused me. They never received this letter for the simple reason that I never sent it to them. It wasn't a question of them knowing how I felt, but rather a question of freeing myself from their hold on my mind, which I refused to acknowledge any longer. My words spoke of forgiveness and gratitude. I let them know that I have, in fact, forgiven their actions. I expressed gratitude that their actions hadn't broken my spirit. Partly because of them, I had become an extremely resilient woman. The path of my destiny became quite clear as peace made its way into my heart. I held my own freedom in my hands. It was up to me to see events for exactly what they were.

I went back to Santorini on my own. I sat on the balcony of the little studio I rented on top of the Albanian's restaurant and had a glass of wine, celebrating my new state of mind for my thirtieth birthday, with an immense feeling of autonomy. I humbly thanked the Greek gods for dropping my angel onto my path when they did, as well as for giving me such a tumultuously exciting life during which I had learned so much about myself and the world.

I returned to Quebec with a new positive energy and outlook, where my continued desire to travel led me to a job with Air Canada Vacations, who sent me to be their representative in my old beloved location of Playa del Carmen, Mexico.

I went back to see my old friend Gus, who had met a new woman and was extremely happy in his new life. I went back because, on my new "vey" that Ralph had constantly urged me to find, I felt that I had to thank the people who had played a crucial role in my past life, and Gus was one of those people. I also went back to where Gigi and I had spent our "honeymoon" stage in the palapas, where I said goodbye to my old life with him and welcomed the new me in once more. I had finally become the woman I always desired to be. I was free.

After Playa del Carmen and Air Canada Vacations, I worked for a time as a receptionist at Club Intrawest at the remarkable Mont-Tremblant ski resort is in the Laurentians, 130 kilometers north of Montreal. I will forever look back at my time there with fondness.

Within a year, I realized that I still had the travel bug buzzing inside me, and that it wanted to have more exciting international adventures as a brand-new woman this time around. I ended up getting an interview with Disney Cruise Line as a cruise staff member.

Working for Disney was a whole new world for me (just like Jasmine and Aladdin), cruising the Caribbean on a magnificent ship called *Magic*. Everything on the ship was out of this world, as was my life on it. My fellow cruise staff members became my friends for life, and soon enough they gave me the nickname of C.C. Dorrie, since I never seemed to grasp their jokes and would stare at them blankly with my big eyes whenever they told one, just like Dory, the endearing fish with a memory problem in *Finding Nemo*. This was a persona which I expanded on as our time together flew by, since it seemed to make my colleagues happy to tease me amicably.

At the end of my contract, I decided to travel the world with another cruise line. My agent contacted me and set me up with the opportunity to work in the boutique of a smaller ship, the *Seven Seas Navigator*, where destiny was waiting to open yet another door for me.

I travelled to the joyful Caribbean, the remarkable Panama Canal, intimidating Columbia, the eerie lands of Iceland, through the colorful yet melancholy scenery of Greenland, froze next to the Polar ice cap in August, saw the Midnight sun beside the sharp, rocky cliffs of the Norwegian coast, visited the majestic Hermitage in Saint Petersburg, walked the beautiful streets of Gdansk, Poland, visited the famous Tivoli Gardens in Copenhagen, walked the humbling cobblestoned alleys of Tallinn, sailed the royal fjords of Norway, saw majestic castles in Ireland and drank a beer in a real Irish pub, experienced medieval Riga, Latvia, and ended up making a full circle back to the Bahamas in 2005.

When Hurricane Katrina devastated New Orleans and a friend of mine, Nicole, asked me to be part of her plan for the Red Cross, I said yes without really thinking about what it might entail. The plan? She decided to throw a fundraiser and use the most popular people on our elegant ship to aid her noble cause, and since I was one of the most coveted girls on the seas back then, she thought I would be of great help.

The fundraiser, an auction titled -Win a Date With...-, actually turned out to be a really fun event. While most of us "went" for around $75, when "win a date with C.C." came up, I ended up being "sold" to the highest bidder for $552 USD. The man who'd "bought" me loved New Orleans so much that he had dedicated a whole paycheck to my friend's honorable cause. It was one of the most romantic things I had ever experienced.

There he was: a tiny, handsome Bulgarian man who would become my whole life and with whom I would create two wonderful little angels of my own. We now live in peace in the foggy Maritimes, right on the ocean.

While what ensued between Ralph and I remains a mystery, I feel that I have finally found my way—and that perhaps this life was waiting for me all along. I just had to follow my destiny's path to find my way home at last.

"Even the darkest night will end and the sun will rise"

Victor Hugo

64743671R00194

Made in the USA
Charleston, SC
11 December 2016